D1195324

THE STRUCTURE OF POETRY

THE STRUCTURE OF POETRY

by

ELIZABETH SEWELL

ROUTLEDGE & KEGAN PAUL LTD
Broadway House, 68–74 Carter Lane, London

First Published in 1951
by Routledge and Kegan Paul Ltd
Broadway House, Carter Lane
London, E.C.4
Second Impression 1962

Printed in Great Britain
by Lowe & Brydone (Printers) Ltd
London, N.W.10

"I should like to have it explained," said the Mock Turtle.

"She can't explain it," hastily said the Gryphon. "Go on to the next verse."

(*Alice in Wonderland.*)

PREFACE

THE mainsprings of this inquiry have been, in poetry, the *Illuminations* and *Bateau Ivre* of Rimbaud and the poems of Mallarmé, particularly the Sonnets and *Un Coup de Dés* ; in prose, Rimbaud's *Une Saison en Enfer* and the *Lettre du Voyant*, Mallarmé's *Divagations* and *La Musique et les Lettres* ; and certain prose works of Valéry, especially the series *Variété I–IV*. A list of works consulted will be found in the bibliography at the end of the book. Passages or ideas drawn from these which have been built into the text have in every case been indicated by footnotes, and where italics occur in quotations, they are those of the author quoted.

Passages in French, where it was the substance rather than the language which mattered, have been given in translation, though the references to editions and pages given in footnotes refer to the original French. Where quotations from Mallarmé's prose occur, I have left the original and put the translation in a footnote, feeling that the original may well be less obscure than my translation. For translations of the poetry, I have made frequent use of Miss Helen Rootham's Translations of the *Illuminations*, and of Mr. Roger Fry's translations of Mallarmé's sonnets. My thanks are due to the publishers, Messrs. Faber and Faber and Messrs. Chatto and Windus respectively, for permission to use the extracts given.

I have called the work *The Structure of Poetry*, but it would perhaps have been more accurate to have called it the construction of a way of thinking about poetry. The general results are summarized at the end of Part I, and the new way of thinking is tried out on Rimbaud and Mallarmé in Part II.

The writer set off with the best intentions of producing a sensible piece of research, but this aim vanished when once the process of thinking for oneself was embarked on, i.e. from

Chapter 4 onwards. After that the only thing to do was, I found, to let each new bit grow out of the one before ; so each chapter should be regarded as a fixing or crystallization of the stage of thought reached at that point, and nothing more. The end and finished system may have been implicit from the start, but the constructor did not know exactly how the last chapters, sometimes even the next chapter, would turn out, and the work was full of surprises and what in honesty I can only call lucky guesses. The choice of Mallarmé and Rimbaud was one of these. I picked on them because I knew they would provide nourishment, and if one has to chew something for three years it is better to chew good food rather than sawdust ; but I had no idea at the beginning how lucky a choice this would prove to be.

During the three years that went to the making of the first version of this, and through all the experiment and guesswork and surprises, I have been blessed with a Supervisor, Dr. L. C. Harmer, of Trinity College, Cambridge, whose support and encouragement never failed. What this meant will be understood by anyone who knows the difficulties, external and internal, that beset work of this sort. He bears, first, my very great gratitude for his understanding and loyalty, and, second, no responsibility whatever for the way of thinking set out here. My thanks are also due to Miss Alison Fairlie and Dr. Werner Brock, whose criticisms of the first version of this work were most helpful.

E. S.

CONTENTS

FIGURES

PART I

1. The Nature of the Inquiry

THE account of Alice's meeting with the Caterpillar in *Wonderland* ends with an excellent description of the predicament of any inquirer confronted with a problem that can apparently be solved only by experiment. Alice is left saying to herself: "One side of *what*? The other side of *what*?" and when the answer turns out to be a mushroom, she still has to decide where to begin, "and as it was perfectly round, she found this a very difficult question." First to establish the *what*, then to proceed to the *how*, seems elementary enough; but the difficulties are very real, and the alarming things that happened to Alice in the course of her experiments may be a warning that the process is not as simple as it might seem.

In this inquiry, the question asked is: What makes language into poetry? Because this is a subject that is far too big to be handled simply in that form, attention will be chiefly directed towards poetry as it appears in the work of two poets, Rimbaud and Mallarmé. The results of the inquiry, however, if they are to be any use, ought to throw some light on the structure of poetry in general. In one sense this is only the second stage, as the statement of the problem shows, for the question "what makes language into poetry?" puts language first, and this is where the inquiry must begin. This also is far too big, and the problem of *how* arises at once, as it would confront an amateur suddenly given the job of cutting up a sperm-whale single-handed. On what method can the thing be divided into manageable pieces? Or, to put the question in more dignified terms: what method of analysis is to be employed?

Perhaps the first step is to see how it can *not* be done. The ordinary mind, groping its way towards a solution, starts probably by regarding language as a stable organization that can be broken up into units (words or phrases), which have real meaning and whose grouping can be investigated by the rules of traditional grammar. Observing language at this level would be like watching a game of football ; it would not occur to the observer to doubt that the little figures in the field were real people, or to question or deny the recognized rules of the game. This unquestioning attitude towards language, however, vanishes after even a short course of reading in linguistics.

First of all, the stable organization turns out to be an illusion. Modern scholars of linguistics insist that the field of action and inquiry must be the shifting ground of the spoken language, not the apparently more stable ground of the written. Secondly, the notion that language can be divided into word-units has to be abandoned in face of the experts' insistence on the practical impossibility of defining the " word " or of using it as a self-contained unit. Then grammar comes in for its turn, and this, too, vanishes in a chorus of disapproval which maintains that traditional grammar is an obsolete survival of medieval scholasticism, that the grammatical categories rest upon no logical basis and that standards of correctness in language are merely misleading, " barricades of cobwebs, . . . police regulations, full of prohibitions, of restrictions, of quibbling." [1] Lastly, the fact that we lend significance to certain groups of sounds and words, assuming that they are capable of imparting something to other people who speak the same tongue, proves to be equally full of difficulties. The notion of " meaning " becomes so thorny that it seems best to avoid the term altogether and fall back on the slightly less dangerous term " reference " instead. Any hope of identifying anything approaching " real meaning " has gone. A little thought makes it plain that there is no direct connection between, for instance, my name and myself. The two are linked together in practice, but the link must go through my mind or another's mind before the connection exists. Language has no direct connection with reality. It is in one sense a double reflection, for man can perceive

[1] Ferdinand Brunot, *La Pensée et la Langue*, Masson et Cie., Éditeurs, Paris, 1922, Introd., p. ix.

external objects only through his senses, defectively at that, and the impression so gained, a personal one, is reflected in language. The original, whatever it may be, is at two removes, as is the face reflected out of one mirror into another. The realization of this may lead to nihilism, to a position which denies any real content and hence any value to language or to thought which is dependent on language. This brings in at once the question of the nature of reality in the external world and the world of thought and ideas, psychology and philosophy in fact ; these must be formally declared to be out of bounds for this inquiry, which has enough to deal with already.

By now the list of methods that are *not* to be employed is growing formidable, but a search for more positive help from the experts does not yield the desired results. Not only each branch of linguistics but each writer on language produces a different system of analysis, a separate way of thinking about language, ranging from Jespersen's division of it into "full" and "empty" words to the distinction between the "symbolic" and "emotive" functions of language put forward by Ogden and Richards in *The Meaning of Meaning* or the extreme complexity of the system of divisions, sub-divisions, and cross-references used by Damourette et Pichon in their work *Des Mots à la Pensée*. These and all the other suggested methods of analysis have this in common, however—they do not provide the means of answering the question : what makes language into poetry ? It is a problem that puts forward an enormous bulk of subject-matter, and the methods of the experts produce nothing but a mass of dismembered pieces, unmanageable except for an expert, and useless for the purpose in hand here.

Some connection has to be established between these two, between the pieces of language with which analytical scholarship works and the finished construction of the poet. There can be no question of rejecting the former method, for it can produce much that is helpful in a study of poetry ; but it is necessary to remember at this stage that the analytical method, the scholar's system, does not constitute an absolute. It is not a pattern to which all thought must

2. The Particular Subject Matter

BY the nature of their art all poets must be concerned with language. The form which this concern takes will vary between two extremes. The first is where language to be used in poetry is handled purely intuitively, and where the problems, if any, are dealt with by intuition also—" Ich singe, wie der Vogel singt, Der in den Zweigen wohnet ",[1] as Goethe says, the native wood-notes wild. The second and opposite pole is the attitude of acute intellectual inquiry (which may go on at the same time as creative poetic work) into language, its nature, and its difficulties as an artistic medium. Perhaps this is something of what Baudelaire had in mind when he wrote, in *L'Art Romantique*, " All the great poets become critics, naturally and fatally." This could be matched by many such statements since, Cyril Connolly's remark, for instance, in his preface to Aragon's *Le Crève-Cœur*, " The poet who is not an intellectual is to-day at a technical disadvantage," or T. S. Eliot's phrase in *East Coker*, " The intolerable wrestle with words and meanings." This rather than the other is the usual attitude towards poetry to-day.

Whether the poet's concern with language be conscious or unconscious, however, it is certainly there, embodied in his work, and so this study could presumably be illustrated by examples from the work of any poet or group of poets, no matter what language they were writing in, since whatever it is that makes language into poetry is not confined to any particular tongue. This means that the choice of any one poet or poetic school must seem arbitrary, French poetry of the late nineteenth century no less so than any other choice. There are the following reasons, however, for choosing this particular poetry as a springboard : it

[1] Lit.—I sing as sings the bird that lives in the branches.

began to do very strange things with language ; for the most part it did them consciously ; and poetry has continued to do them in greater or lesser degree ever since. From this period, two poets, Rimbaud and Mallarmé, have been singled out for special study, partly because they illustrate the three characteristics just mentioned, but still more because they are great enough to convince the mind that though it does not understand them, there is something there, infinitely worth discovering if only one can reach it. First, however, it is important to see them in their historical setting, lest they should seem two freaks from whose tamperings with language no general conclusions can fairly be drawn.

The period spanned by their works, roughly 1870–1900, saw in France the gradual decline of the Parnassian school of poetry, with its insistence on outward forms and its erudite vocabulary, and the rise of the Symbolist school, which one of its members, Gustave Kahn, describes in this way : " The bond between the symbolists, apart from an undeniable love of art, and a fellow-feeling for the literary misfits of the preceding age, consisted above all in a wholesale negation of former practice." [1] It was a rather nebulous collection of poetic innovators, and neither Rimbaud nor Mallarmé, nor the third great poet of the period, Verlaine, can properly be said to belong to it. It forms the background, however, temporal or spiritual, against which the work of Mallarmé was written ; Rimbaud's work was produced earlier, but belongs nowhere.

The contemporary criticism, particularly the work of Lemaître, Brunetière, Catulle Mendès, and Anatole France, provides for those who are interested a lively commentary on these poetic developments. In 1889 an essay of Lemaître was published in which he says : " I believe this to be the first time that writers have seemed to be unaware of the traditional meaning of words, and, in the combinations of them, of the very genius itself of the French tongue ; and have made up a kind of hocus-pocus absolutely unintelligible not merely to ordinary people, but to the most shrewd

[1] *Symbolistes et Décadents*, Vanier, Paris, 1902, p. 51.

men of letters."[1] The statement that it was the first time such a thing had happened is probably rather too sweeping, and Lemaître himself, in an essay written ten years earlier, had complained of the "jargon" of certain Parnassian poets.[2] It is near enough to the truth, however, to be interesting, because something strange does seem to have happened to poetry about this time, and Lemaître recognizes this. Exactly what it was is not clear yet, but may come to light later. Meantime, a few examples follow of the innovations, experiments, and obscurities which produced such remarks as those of Lemaître.

> Mirage colore, fragrance
> De jeunes jardins et de carrefour rance ;
> Doux frôler susurre comme d'une source,
> Râper anxieux comme d'une étoffe rebourse :
> Il est un Monstre.[3]
>
> (From *Le Pélerin Passionné*, Moréas.)

> Nuits — de vorations
> cillaires, en dïaprures d'inquiétudes :
> d'indures plissements d'oesophages, de leur
> innervation péri-staltique qui élonge
> reptaient l'annelé ventre des Verminations
> dont vident en vie aveugle leurs plénitudes
> les marées salant les eaux de l'Intérieur.[4]
>
> (From *Dire Du Mieux*, René Ghil.)

> Dolosive, intensive ruse des ailes des papillons d'antan
> à quel heurt des jours leurrants, l'instinct du temps,
> La nuit plane et sur les sommeils défaille

[1] *Les Contemporains*, 4e Série, Lecène et Oudin, Paris, 1889, p. 65.

[2] *Les Contemporains*, 8e Série, Paris, 1918, p. 39.

[3] I translate literally :—

> Coloured mirage, fragrance
> Of young gardens and rancid crossroads ;
> Gentle stroking whispers like a spring,
> Anxious rasping as of an intractable stuff :
> He (it) is a Monster.

[4]
> Nights—of cillary
> vorations, in mottlings of anxieties :
> from hardened foldings of oesophaguses, from their
> peri-staltic innervation which stretches out
> the ringed belly crawled the Verminations
> from which empty their fulnesses in blind life
> the tides salting the waters of the Interior.

repos des exilés du rêve, de ceux à sa taille
repos inéclos aux pas assourdis de qui sait le temps
Ah ! courbe sous tes paupières
lourdes de mémoires de pierres
gisantes où voulurent les parallèles hasards.[1]
(From *Les Palais Nomades*, Kahn.)

...ce doit être
le Septentrion aussi Nord
UNE CONSTELLATION
froide d'oubli et de désuétude
pas tant
qu'elle n'énumère
sur quelque surface vacante et supérieure
le heurt successif
sidéralement
d'un compte total en formation...[2]
(From *Un Coup de Dés*, Mallarmé.)

Un vert et un bleu très foncés envahissent l'image. Dételage aux environs d'une tache de gravier.

— Ici va-t-on siffler pour l'orage, et les Sodomes et les Solymes, et les bêtes féroces et les armées.

(Postillon et bêtes de songe, reprendront-ils sous les plus suffocantes futaies, pour m'enfoncer jusqu'aux yeux dans la source de soie ?)

[1] Deceptive, intensive ruse of the wings of the butterflies of former time
to what shock of the luring days, the instinct of time,
The night floats and on the slumbers faints
repose of the exiled of dream, of those of its stature
repose in bud with the deadened footsteps of who knows the time
Ah ! curved beneath thine eyelids
heavy with memories of stones
lying where the parallel hazards wished.

[2] . . . this should be
the Septentrion also North
A CONSTELLATION
cold with forgetfulness and lack of use
not so much
that it does not number out
on some vacant and superior surface
the successive shock
starrily
of a sum total in formation. . . .

Et nous envoyer, fouettés à travers les eaux clapotantes et les boissons répandues, rouler sur l'aboi des dogues...
— Un souffle disperse les limites du foyer.[1]

(From *Les Illuminations*, Rimbaud.)

Faced with this sort of thing, it is no wonder that one man of letters after another joined in the chorus of bewilderment and indignation. Jules Huret's *Enquête sur l'Évolution Littéraire*,[2] which gives reports of interviews with all the leading literary figures of the time, is full of explosions: "Complete eclipse of French, of lucidity, of common sense! Astounding, an aberration like this! And this language! Look, just take a hat, throw into it adverbs, conjunctions, prepositions, nouns, adjectives, pick them out haphazard and write them down: there's symbolism for you." "They overturn the language from top to bottom, without rhyme or reason, and they claim that that's evocative!"[3] "These Symbolo-Decadent-Instrumento-Gagaïsts, for whom French isn't good enough and who replace it by a laboured double-dutch."[4] It seems plain that to these men at any rate such experiments with the language of poetry were something new—and unheard-of, in every sense.

The experimenters were clear about this themselves. The need for renewal, both in the language itself and in its organization in poetry, is emphasized again and again, and numerous theoretical works on poetry were produced during this period by the poets themselves, showing that they approached these problems of language in full consciousness. This was one more nail in their coffin as far as the critics were concerned, who could not forgive the apparently deliberate nature of what to them was double-dutch. It has advantages, however, for this inquiry. The fact that the

[1] "—Deep blues and greens invade the picture. The horses are unharnessed near a gravel pit.
—At this point someone will whistle for thunderstorms, Sodoms and Solymas, and savage beasts and armies.
(Will this dream postilion and these dream horses drag me into a stifling forest, in order to plunge me up to the eyes in a silken stream?)
And, flogging the horses through splashing waters and spilled drinks, send us rolling along while dogs are barking. . . .
—A breath of wind disperses the landmarks of the homestead."

(Translation by Helen Rootham.)

[2] Bibliothèque Charpentier, Paris, 1913.
[3] Leconte de Lisle, pp. 279 and 282.
[4] Laurent Tailhade, p. 328.

obscurity in the poetry is deliberate should make it easier to investigate than if it were the product of chance, whilst besides the poetry the theoretical writing can be referred to as well. This is so with both Rimbaud and Mallarmé. Rimbaud provides a commentary on his life and poetical method in *Une Saison En Enfer*, as well as in the earlier letter known as the *Lettre Du Voyant*, while Mallarmé wrote a number of prose works on literary questions ; the student of these must not be deterred by the fact that at first sight they appear, if anything, more obscure even than Mallarmé's poetry.

On the third point originally made—that since this period poetry has to a greater or lesser degree continued to do strange things with language—little can be said here, not because the point is unimportant but because it is too important. The persistence of obscurity in poetry down to the present day is an observable fact. So, too, is the continuing influence of Rimbaud and Mallarmé in this country as well as in France. These two points cannot be discussed here, but they are mentioned because they suggest that if some way of thinking can be found that will illuminate the obscurity of these two, it may explain other things than just a tendency in French poetry some fifty years ago.

3. The Starting-point

SOME plan of action is necessary in any enterprise, even in one as indeterminate as this is at present, consisting as it does of nothing yet except a search for a way of thinking. A simple plan would be the best ; but by the end of Chapter 1 the suspicion had already arisen that a double plan of action or a dual way of thinking might be unavoidable. So the fact that two plans suggest themselves need not mean that the inquiry is going off the rails.

Both plans have to do with language, and throughout this work the term " language " will apply only to word-languages, not to such other languages as music or algebra, for instance, with which poetry is not concerned. Despite the objections, there seems nothing for it at present but to employ the term " word " and to use it for the time being as a unit to think with where a unit is unavoidable, provided it is understood that it is used without being defined, i.e. without being boxed in in any way, and if either writer or reader finds it easier to think in terms of phrases or other groupings of language, he or she is at liberty to do so. The mind does something of the sort when working on a poem, and poetry is after all the goal of this inquiry.

The first plan is to think of language, or of words, as consisting of two parts, two halves, a division as artificial as the division of a human being into body and spirit and not unlike it. I propose to call these two aspects of language " sound-look " and " reference ". Sound-look is the outward shape of a word, in letters or sounds, the up-and-down and in-and-out of strokes on some surface as seen by the eye or by the mind's eye, and the series of noises represented by these and picked up by the ear or imagined in silence in the head. The other aspect of language is reference. This term is used here to cover everything that happens in the mind when a word, as sound-look, is seen, heard, spoken, or thought. Strictly speaking, this is a more general use of the term than is technically permissible. This aspect of language is usually split up into two divisions, by Vendryes, for instance, who calls them "affectif" and "logique" (*Le Langage*, p. 163), or by Ogden and Richards (*The Meaning of Meaning*, p. 149), who speak of the symbolic function of language, i.e. the recording and communication of references, and the emotive, evocative of feelings and attitudes. This particular way of thinking, involving a distinction between intellect and emotion, will not be adopted here, because emotion is an irrelevance in a work of construction, and it is the *structure* of poetry that is in question. Nor will other faculties of the brain, such as imagination, or the "conscious" and "subconscious", be separated in thought and discussed individually. They are not facts (a point we tend to forget); they are only ways of thinking and not convenient here. I am proposing to take a rough and ready view of the head as something inside which all kinds of things happen, but which can and must be regarded as a whole. So reference, from now on, will signify the effect of a word on this whole, the impact of a word in the head, as Valéry says.

This is the first plan for a way of thinking: words as (*a*) sound-look, (*b*) reference.

The second plan works in a different dimension, so that instead of language being divided up according to certain qualities it will be divided according to quantity. It is as follows: (*a*) words as individuals; (*b*) words in small groups; (*c*) words in larger groups making a whole, e.g. a poem. This, too, is only a convenient way of thinking, and this three-fold division has no linguistic or philosophic significance. It should provide a starting-point, however, and that point will be stage (*a*), words as individuals, because some way of thinking about these will have to be found which can lead on to the next stage, and so, finally, to poetry. It is no use beginning with the last and imagining one can break poetry up into individual words and then study it. The only thing to do is to recognize that the point has now been reached at which the jump from the spring-board must be made, the point where the manuals of instruction cease to be any use and the amateur must begin to proceed on his own, as if no one had ever done it before and as if all the experts did not exist. It may be a fact that words cannot be treated as individuals, but it will lead nowhere to accept this on second-hand evidence, for in the process of looking at words as individuals something may emerge that will help to show what holds them together, and so a scaffolding could be built up by which to climb to the next stage of the argument and so, building up the way of thinking as seems best, to the last stage, which is poetry. The experts will provide hand-hold and foot-hold time and again, but to expect them to build for another's private purpose would be unreasonable ; nor can they do the climbing—that would be unseemly.

Although the eventual aim is poetry, and both these plans are framed with that in view, it will be necessary to begin with language in its ordinary use and to see how the normal mind's view of experience, embodied in the ordinary use of language, differs from that of the poet. It may be said that the normal person uses language as he uses money : it is something to be taken wholly for granted. This is very likely true, but all the same it seems probable that language, which is so closely fused with thought as to be considered by some to be identical with it, must reflect the mind's way of looking at reality, the common basis of day-to-day human life—and it is this which will be covered by the terms "reality" or "experience" from now on. For obvious reasons I am not going to define either. In the minds of ordinary people, reality consists of immediate surroundings and things such as bright colours, warmth, good food, and good company. This is not the physicist's reality, nor the philosopher's, but it is the reality, or the working notion of it, that most people live with. It seems likely, however, that the mind for its own greater convenience splits up reality, or rather its perception of it ; and this, too, language may be expected to reflect. Once this has been investigated it should be possible to see how far the poet in his use of language departs from normal usage and upsets the normally accepted patterns of experience.

Bertrand Russell, in a recent article, remarks : " One may say broadly : all that passes for knowledge can be arranged in a hierarchy of degrees of certainty, with arithmetic and the facts of perception at the top." [1] Possibly words have a similar hierarchy, being grouped in the ordinary mind into broad classes according to that mind's comprehension and organization of its perceptions and ideas. This grouping will, in its turn, affect what may be called a word's power of resistance. On the positive side, the more definite the image or concept called up by a word in the ordinary mind, the greater powers of resistance that word will have, i.e. the word and its special reference will hold closely together, and if the poet desires to shift that reference, he must first break down the word's power of resistance. There may also be a negative form of resistance in words, cases where they will prove intransigent material not because they have definite content for the mind but because they have little or none. Why this resistance should need to be broken is a question that will have to be left till later. Clearly nothing can be done with words as individuals. If in the middle of a sentence on this page I put the word " bread ", that word brings with it inevitably its own particular reference, whether I like it or not ; but with words in groups things may begin to happen, and it is with these that a poet works.

This is one system of connections which may be broken in poetry. Language, too, has its own technical system of connections or relationships, which may also be broken ; but that need not be the end of the process, for all the relationship-systems by which the mind endeavours to make sense of life can presumably also be broken by poetry, in so far as they are embodied in language. Ogden and Richards quote the following relationships as basic : " They are those which we must know and unerringly recognize if we are to survive—similarity, causation, space, and time " (*The Meaning of Meaning*, p. 127). It may be necessary to add to these ; number may have to come in, and also certain deductions from experience, such as, for instance, that particular things have certain invariable qualities. These

[1] *Philosophy for Laymen*, Universities Quarterly, November, 1946, vol. 1, no. 1, p. 45.

systems, however, could be broken. Even in ordinary everyday experience this happens, in dreams and in what makes us laugh. Perhaps it happens in poetry as well.

All kinds of questions begin to arise now : how this may link up with the view of art as a system of purely formal relations ; how far poetry, like the dream, should be beautiful or terrifying or funny but perhaps not sense ; how far the poet's task has to be one of destruction before he can make all things new. This is to anticipate, however, for this will be Stage 2 or Stage 3 of the inquiry. Stage 1 must begin with an examination of words and the ways in which they are used by the mind, for this is basic to the whole problem. This, then, is the starting-point.

4. Words as Individuals

THE first question to be considered is the connection between normal experience and the normal use of language; there is one approach to this which opens up wide and interesting fields and seems the best point at which to begin—the balance between diversity and unity.

Experience as we know it, whether it seems to have its origin outside or inside ourselves, is exceedingly diverse. The mere fact of existing faces us daily, hourly, and momently with a mass of sensations, bodily and otherwise. This diversity needs no emphasis; it is a fact of anyone's experience. To the mind there falls the task of organizing this diversity at various levels, of seizing a moment or a stage in this constant flux and regarding that as a unit to which a term in language can apply. Whether this crystallization of experience at a given point is entirely dependent on language for its functioning or not, language is of the greatest possible help in the mind's task of ordering potential chaos, of bringing unity into diversity.

This organization of diverse experience into something orderly is made possible by certain assumptions, one of the most important being that of similarity. We make the assumption, for practical purposes, that each individual remains essentially the same all the time, i.e. that in life as we know it a banker's clerk descending from a bus is not going to turn into a hippopotamus before our eyes, and that when I wake up to-morrow morning I shall be the same person as I am now (Rimbaud's remark, "Je est *un autre*" [literally, "'I' is *another*"], from the *Lettre du Voyant*, runs counter to this). We assume that things, people, situations, ideas which we perceive to be alike (we do not question our perceptions) *are* alike, and alike for others as well as for ourselves, that " the violet smells to him as it doth to me ", and a violet will be the same in a wood twenty miles away or in a spring time twenty years ahead. In ordinary life we regard this as absolute. At one end it rules out magic and miracle, at the other end it rules out incoherence and madness. It is only an assumption, but it lends stability to an otherwise terrifyingly fluid existence.

In language also, as in life, we make a similar assumption of stability. It is assumed that every word has a stable connection with its object of reference, and that if I say " cow " here and now, or next week, or Mr. X says it instead of me, it will bear the same connection each time with its referent ; it will not refer next week, or in Mr. X's mouth, to a waste paper basket or a Cabinet Minister. Experience, as we know, is for the most part outside our control, and there are disturbing cases where our assumptions of stability in the world of experience have appeared to be wrong. Language, on the other hand, is, we believe, within our control ; it is man-made and is what man makes of it. For this reason if for no other, the stable connection between word and reference is very tough.

If we think about it at all we know that language changes with time, though we tend to ignore this unless brought face to face with an example such as the Collect in the Prayer Book which begins : " Prevent us, O Lord, in all our doings with Thy most gracious favour." This can be paralleled in the world of real life by the experience of looking at a photograph of one's own face taken perhaps ten years ago, when the change which in practice we ignore or cannot perceive because of its gradualness, " the unimaginable touch of time," is made plain by the crystallization of something, here one's own features, at a given point. The mutability of language, as of everything within our experience, we choose to ignore ; but the stability of language in the connection between word and referent is practically absolute. Any word is not interchangeable with any other. There are certain cases of exchange, near-synonymity, or substitution, but these follow rules of their own, in general well understood. Maud Budden's Clerihew is a case in point :—

" Why
Do the very young apply
The word for a practitioner of necromancy
To any object that takes their fancy ? "

But this might be called a strictly temporary Agreement to Differ. Apart from such minor departures from convention, I know very well that I cannot say " cow " when I mean something else. " This belief in what almost amounts to a pre-established harmony corresponds with a profound need of our being—the need for equilibrium and synthesis " (Bally).[1]

So we have an unlimited diversity of experience with relative stability imposed on it at certain levels of organization (according to the greater or lesser degree of complexity in the reference) with the help of language. We take the stability of the world of experience to be absolute in our normal thinking ; the stability of language is absolute for all practical purposes. So the mind orders chaos and labels it—and we have the intelligible world in which we live. But there is more to it than this. Valéry touches on it when he says : " But the constructor whom I now put forward takes for chaos and for raw material precisely that world-order which the Demiurge has extracted from primal disorder. The forms of nature already exist ; but something bids him consider the work as unfinished, needing to be remoulded and set in movement again, so as to prove more satisfying to man in particular." [2] So the poet, the artist whose chosen medium is words, takes as raw material, as chaos, precisely that finished system of organization of the facts of experience which the normal mind achieves with the help of language. That the system is supposed to be finished and presents a workable whole means nothing to him. It is all relative. The point of crystallization is arbitrary at whatever level it occurs, and the reasonably tidy organization of diverse experience achieved by the mind is arbitrary too. Each whole, each unity imposed by the mind upon diversity carries with it the principle of its own dissolution,

[1] *Linguistique générale et Linguistique française*, Leroux, Paris, 1932, Introd., p. 9.

[2] Paul Valéry, *Eupalinos ou l'Architecte*, NRF, Gallimard, Paris, 1924, p. 215.

for each thing presupposes its opposite, intellectually speaking, and a unity presupposes disunity or diversity again. The total synthesis, which would impose unity on diversity without further appeal, is not humanly possible. Each synthesis, large or small, which brings stability is only the holding of a balance, a momentary equilibrium between unity and diversity.

This balancing process as seen in the use of language can be looked at under five main heads.

(1) Stable word + stable reference (unity without diversity).
(2) Stable word + stabilized diversity of reference.
(3) Stable word + unstabilized diversity of reference.
(4) Stable word + absence of reference.
(5) Unstable word + impossibility of reference.

(1) *Stable Word + Stable Reference.*

This is the scientist's ideal for language ; in practice it is difficult to obtain. Into this group come technical terms which have not become absorbed into the vocabulary of ordinary life, and so retain a precise and undifferentiated meaning. In this group also belong words of number. The scientific term implies diversity in that it is probably the result of the deductive method of reasoning, which supposes a diversity of data ; number also by its nature implies diversity—but in each case the diversity has been unified by the intellect, and the unit so achieved is final, or practically so, and therefore stable.

It is interesting that number possesses a dual system of notation, that of words and that of digits, and perhaps there is a greater significance in this than just the question of convenience. Written language in general and poetry in particular avoid the use of digits.

The larger the number, the more likely it is to get outside this group and into another less stable one, for in such cases the mind can only maintain stability by clinging to the name of the number, so to speak, and ignoring the diversity ; eventually the sense of diversity becomes so acute that the mind cannot cope with it any longer, and the word would then find itself in another group where the stable word remains but where the stability of the reference, or perhaps the presence of any reference at all, has vanished. One often hears people say : " The numbers are so vast they don't mean anything." In this connection it is interesting to note the following remark in Valéry's *Monsieur Teste* : " Monsieur Teste spoke about money. . . . Eight hundred and ten million seventy-five thousand five hundred and fifty. . . . I was listening to this strange music without following the calculation. It imparted to me the tremors of the Stock Exchange, and the long series of names of numbers possessed me like a poem." [1]

Words in this group are going to be very resistant to any kind of imaginative or artistic, as distinct from intellectual, employment. From the purely intellectual point of view they are models of precision. (It should be noted that apart from sound-look they are for the most part without emotive power.[2]) There is no emotive power in the " Pyrola uniflora " that occurs in Stephen Spender's *Polar Exploration*, for example, or in the " quinze mille pieds de diamètre " (fifteen thousand feet in diameter), from Rimbaud's *Villes II* in the *Illuminations*. Words in this group have a rock-like integrity, by the very fact that there is no diversity in their reference ; should diversity creep in, then their status as technical terms belonging to this group is weakened in exact proportion to it.

(2) *Stable Word + Stabilized Diversity of Reference.*

The balance here between unity and diversity is not static but it is reasonably stable. It is the balance of the see-saw which may swing first one way and then the other, and individual minds will vary in the degree of stability ascribed to any particular reference. Balance seems to be most satisfactorily achieved where the diversity falls within the bounds of sense perception and where the mind has succeeded in crystallizing the reference into a unity. Rimbaud is a remarkable repository of words of this kind. Examples which may be found in his work, particularly the *Illuminations*,

[1] NRF, Gallimard, Paris, 1927, pp. 44–5.
[2] Ogden and Richards, op. cit., ch. vi, p. 131, " . . . the lack of emotive power which is a peculiarity of all technicalities."

consist of ordinary names for particular kinds of animals, birds, plants, minerals, food and drink, weather, natural phenomena, external parts of the body where there is no very great personal differentiation, buildings and constructions, including their component parts and contents, machinery, everyday apparatus such as clothes, umbrellas, musical instruments and furniture, and materials such as different kinds of wood or woven stuffs.

Other types of words besides names come into this group too, but to qualify they need to be what one might call " matter-of-fact ". The reference may be complex and usually is, being composed of a considerable diversity of elements ; on looking into such a word as " bread ", for instance, one becomes aware of the complexity of the reference, which is a mixture of sight, smell, taste, feel (varying from the feel of a loaf in the hand to the feel of the texture of bread in the mouth), not to mention the word's associations or the sound-look aspect. The reference may even be unfamiliar to us at first-hand. Take, for instance, the bear who makes an appearance in *Bottom* or the volcano of *Barbare* in the *Illuminations*. We may not live on terms of familiarity with bears or volcanoes, but this within certain limits does not matter ; what does matter is that we should have sufficient diversity of material to give the reference substance, and sufficient unification of the image for it to be clear in the mind, assuming rightly or wrongly that one bear does not differ much from another. A very great familiarity with all sorts of bears would lift the word out of this category of certainty and bring it more under the heading of class-words, where our own words " cat " and " dog " have gone. Total unfamiliarity with bears, on the other hand, would either shift the word into Group 1 among the technical terms or into Group 4 where there is no reference at all.

Where the balance is satisfactorily held, words in this group make up a world where things are definite without being too much so, where Verlaine's " un oiseau sur l'arbre qu'on voit " is a thrush singing in a plane-tree, but not a *Turdus ericetorum ericetorum.* Words and references in this group are the common property of everyone within a common civilization, and allowing for certain variations in geography or degree of material culture, they are the common property of humanity. They are what we grow up with. They are the chief ingredient in fairy story and folk tale, and, coming over into the world of poetry, in nursery rhyme ; this is a world of green and blue lavender, of strawberries, sugar, and cream, of brown hair tied up with a bunch of blue ribbons, of a cat down a well, mice and carving knives, rings on fingers and bells on toes, snowy north winds and robins in barns, curds and whey and a great spider, a king and three fiddlers, a queen eating bread and honey, and so on and on.

In certain types of poetry, too, as well as in nursery rhyme, they play a very great part, sometimes to the exclusion of almost everything else (apart from sound-look which is always present). Half a dozen examples drawn at random in time and place may serve as illustration :—

" The sails were of the taffetie
And the masts o' the beaten gold."

(From the ballad, *The Demon Lover.*)

" Here are cool mosses deep,
And thro' the moss the ivies creep,
And in the stream the long-leaved flowers weep,
And from the craggy ledge the poppy hangs in sleep."

(Tennyson, *The Lotos Eaters.*)

" Gently I stir a white feather fan,
With open shirt sitting in a green wood.
I take off my cap and hang it on a jutting stone ;
The wind from the pine tree trickles on my bare head."

(Arthur Waley, from the Chinese of Li Po.)

" With a cargo of ivory,
And apes and peacocks,
Sandalwood, cedarwood, and sweet white wine."

(Masefield, *Cargoes.*)

" Have you felt the wool of beaver ?
Or swans down ever ?
Or have smelt o' the bud o' the briar
Or the nard in the fire,
Or have tasted the bag of the bee ? "

(Ben Jonson, *The Triumph.*)

" Who is she that looketh forth as the morning,
Fair as the moon,
Clear as the sun,
And terrible as an army with banners ? "
(*The Song of Solomon*, Authorized Version.)

The supply of examples of this sort is unfailing, and the pleasure in them is unfailing, too, for there can be great joy and satisfaction in the handling of this group of words, be it active or passive. Perhaps this is because they are concerned with the tangible world of which man is reasonably sure, or because the mind has had the greatest measure of success here in creating stability, in holding the balance between diversity and unity. The system of bringing order from chaos by crystallizing the latter at certain points is at its best here, and the satisfaction of this group may lie in a sense of power. The words themselves are powerful, too ; their resistance differs in kind from that of words in Group 1, but it is none the less strong. One single word of this type set in a poem where otherwise this group is avoided will affect the mind strongly. An example of this is the sestet in Mallarmé's poem which begins " Surgi de la croupe et du bond ", where the last line with its sudden living reality, " Une rose dans les ténèbres " (a rose in the darkness), produces an effect almost physical. Even in complete isolation, in so far as words can be, they will assert themselves, as in " O palmes ! diamant ! " (O palms ! diamond !) from *Angoisse* in the *Illuminations*. A poet may seek them out, as Rimbaud does in so many cases, or may avoid them ; but the reasons for this, as well as the uses that may be made of them, must wait until the time comes to consider words in relationships.

Only certain words in this group approximate to a perfect balance between unity and diversity. Indeed, the dividing line between one group and another is anything but hard and fast, and individual people will almost certainly vary in the words which they would assign to the groups. So, in this group, after the words we have been considering, there come others where the diversity is already beginning to encroach on the stability of the image, until finally the reference becomes completely unstable, when the word would not belong here but in Group 3. There are, however, three subdivisions of this present group to be considered before that stage is reached.

(*a*) Words where the reference holds diversity within itself by nature ; by which I mean, in its simplest form, something that changes perceptibly as you look at it. In real life there are not many of these Protean forms ; the main ones seem to be concerned with light, fire, and water, giving rise to such words as : sea, clouds, sky, flame. The difficulty of stabilizing the image is partly overcome by crystallizing the impression at different stages, in which case the total reference becomes almost a class-word, " his sea in no showing the same, his sea and the same 'neath each showing," as Kipling says in *The Sea and the Hills*. Change is the lot of all earthly things, but mostly they change slowly enough for each stage of development to be easily crystallized into language, " fruit, thorn, and flower," for instance in De la Mare's *Berries*, or the words for the phases of the moon.

(*b*) Those words where the image is so familiar and so diverse that unification is difficult, or is only possible at the abstract level of classification. When I say a word like " room " or " street ", the reference, if I have time to think, is not static but cinematographic. All sorts of possible rooms and streets present themselves to my mind, and the diversity tends to win the day.

(*c*) Class-words, such as " tree " or " animal ". Here also the potential diversity in the reference prevents stability except at an intellectual level. The difficulty is exemplified in the words of the song :—

> " The animals went in two by two,
> The elephant and the kangaroo,"

where we are only too well aware of the dissimilarities. The word remains stable, but the reference tends towards the abstract, and the unity, such as it is, is largely verbal.

Words within these three subgroups, where the balance of unity and diversity in the reference is wavering, will offer resistance of a different kind from that of words where the balance is steadier. As diversity gains over unity, the personality of the word is weakened, and possibly its powers of association are affected, too. The stable word remains, but the equilibrium in the reference is going or gone. This leads on to the next group.

(3) *Stable Word with Unstabilized Diversity of Reference.*

Words in this group come under the general heading of abstracts, for the good reason that in everyday life it is impossible to live with unstabilized diversity ; the mind has to unify or " make sense " of its impressions somehow. But with abstracts this urgency disappears and, in any case, stable unification is difficult here. Ogden and Richards draw attention to the confusions that continually ensue through lack of understanding of this group of words, and say : " Why language is often so recalcitrant to growth at these points is a puzzling problem.' Just possibly part of the answer to this may be that the mind's need to bring unity out of diversity is so great that it will cling to the fictitious unity imposed on a number of notions by a single word such as " truth ". The unity is only verbal, but perhaps to the mind even this is better than nothing, a façade over chaos. The trouble here is that the façade is wearing thin, being of words and nothing else.

Words in this group will not present the poet with the unyielding resistance of words in Group 1, nor with the precarious and shifting equilibrium of words in Group 2 ; but they have powers of resistance of their own, as a featherbed has. In a great number of cases they are expert in passive resistance, being both characterless and unhelpful.

(4) *Stable Word with Absence of Reference.*

There are two main groups of word here.

(*a*) Moribund words which through sheer overwork have lost their reference, as the image of royalty is worn off a penny by overmuch thumbing. The loss of reference may not be total, but in many cases it is very nearly so.

(*b*) The " outils grammaticaux ", or grammatical tools. Writers on language do not regard these as words at all, but as morphemes, on a level with such things as suffixes.

The ordinary mind, however, regards them as belonging to the general group of words. Their combination of stable word plus absence of reference results in absolute resistance ; one can do nothing with these except use them as they are meant to be used or decide to leave them out. The absence of diversity brings us back in a circle almost to Group 1 ; there language gives way to sign notation, i.e. to mathematics ; here language has become sound without reference, and can give way equally to another form of sign notation, that of music.

It is helpful in any case to regard these four main groups of words as a circle, or nearly so, because Group 5 is of a different kind altogether. On looking first at the circle of Groups 1 to 4 and then at Group 5 an interesting point comes to light : that language, like intellectual societies, will tolerate petrifaction among members but will not tolerate madness.

(5) *Instability of Language, with Impossibility of Reference.*

Unlike the other four groups, this does not exist in practice ; in fact, it must never exist if what we consider normal life is to carry on, for it would make nonsense of everything. If one word can mean anything at all, then there is nothing to hold on to. All equilibrium has gone because there is only diversity and no unity of any sort. It produces chaos without possibility of order, and isolation without possibility of communication. It is not the world of dream and imagination and " nonsense ",[1] but that of nightmare and terror and madness. If, indeed, language is the only thing that stands between us and chaos, then the extreme conservatism of society as regards its language is understandable ; like Blondin, we cross Niagara Falls on one small rope.

[1] Cf. De la Mare, *Lewis Carroll*, Faber and Faber, Ltd., London, 1932, p. 61. " Dreaming is another state of being with laws as stringent *and* as elastic as those of the world of nonsense."

5. Words as Individuals in Ordinary Life and in Poetry

IN the previous chapter I have been working on the assumption that words could be isolated and roughly classified. This is part of my own process of bringing unity out of diversity, but though I have attempted to organize my subject matter at this point, choosing for a moment to regard words as individual units, this is only a temporary breathing space. It is far easier to think in terms which may be classified and organized rather than in terms of a system of relationships. It is on the first of these two patterns that we live our ordinary lives, and if we were to stop here, we might consider ourselves in possession of a tidy, comprehensible world consisting of simple units to which names have been given, where a spade is called a spade, and where everything does not run into everything else. Working outwards from ourselves, we regard ourselves and all other facts of experience as simple units in a pattern, as if life were a mosaic, a collection of simple and single things.

Language plays a great part in this process, and the ordinary mind regards language as it regards experience, as a collection of single and simple things, i.e. words, which may be arranged in certain patterns—the mosaic again. This is probably inevitable, given the urge to simplify and order the facts of experience. In the process of achieving order out of chaos in our minds, words act as a crystallizing agent, and we have (or think we have) a single word applied to a single reference. We assume that experience can be ordered and simplified into simple units, because life would not be possible for man without this assumption, and this means that we make a similar assumption about language. If language, too, is like life in its raw form, a network of relationships, then our efforts to bring order out of experience by the help of language are doomed to failure ; we shall merely be trying to express one system of relationships in terms of another. And in point of fact, that is exactly what we are doing. The simplification of each system is an illusion, for the self-contained unit does not exist, either in life or in language.

It may be argued that in the experience of everyday life words can exist in isolation, unaccompanied by other words and untrammelled by relationships. A number of examples come to the mind : "hullo," "help !" "hush," "damn !" my own name perhaps called from upstairs. All of these seem to be capable of existing entirely on their own. (I am excluding "yes" and "no" and answers to the simplest forms of question because they are responses to other words and not therefore in isolation.) It is worth noticing, however, that these isolated words could without loss to communication or to the desired effect be translated into inarticulate sound, which is not language, or one stage further into gesture, i.e. they could, by being expressed in sound or movement, pass out of language altogether. "Help !" for instance, could be a wordless scream or a wild waving of the arms, or both. "Hush" could be a sibilant hiss or a finger on the lips, while "damn" could be a growl or a stamping foot, or, in extreme stress, a hurling to the ground of the nearest breakable, or physical violence upon the offending object. We seem to be at the very edge of language here, where it is almost ceasing to be language. It looks as if those words which in ordinary life occur in isolation do so by virtue of the fact that they are ceasing to be language and are merging into other and more primitive methods of communication. It is perhaps also worth noticing that even these words which occur in isolation very frequently appear in twos or threes rather than singly. There are dozens of possible examples :—

"Hark ! hark ! the lark at heaven's gate sings."
(Shakespeare.)

"Farewell, farewell ! but this I tell
To thee, thou Wedding-Guest !"
(Coleridge.)

"Mary! Mary! *Mary*!
Come to the dairy please!"

(De la Mare.)

"'Help! help! and rescue!' Piglet cried."

(A. A. Milne.)

"So better go on with your work:
But Boys! O Boys! O Boys!"

(St. John Gogarty.)

It may also seem possible in ordinary life to isolate a single reference in the mind, at any rate if the word is concrete and not abstract, to think of "ship" for instance, the thought being unattended by any relation with anything else. Further thought and observation show, however, that any attempt at such isolation in the mind is a hopeless undertaking. The brain is so untidy, subject to continuous activity of widely varying kinds, and never, in the waking state at any rate, completely at rest. "Make your mind a blank," is for the ordinary mind, as everyone knows, an impossible command. And as far as words are concerned, certain discoveries of psycho-analysis, such as the total suppression of a word where the reference causes emotional disturbance, or the significance of word-association, suggest that the system of relationships to which words in the mind belong is very intricate, and that far from being isolated, the word has relationships that go so deep that we are not consciously aware of them.

There are, as everyone knows, occasional words or small phrases which appear to arise in isolation in the mind, like a bubble from the bottom of a pool. Mallarmé describes such an occurrence in *Le Démon de l'Analogie* in the *Divagations*, when he suddenly found himself possessed by the words "La Pénultième est morte" (the Penultimate is dead), "accursed fragments of an absurd phrase," as he himself says. This would seem, however, to be an experience similar to that of getting a tune on the brain. It generally happens with unfamiliar words, often with proper names; I remember being haunted for days by the name

" Merodach-Baladan ", and this may be partly what is at the back of poems about names :—

> " Chimborazo, Cotopaxi
> Took me by the hand,"
>
> (W. J. Turner, *Romance*.)

and others of this kind. Unfamiliarity and resonance produce this result (so that if we go round murmuring something to ourselves all day it will most likely not be, as in the case of the White Queen, " Bread-and-butter, bread-and-butter,") ; but it is not an argument for considering words as individuals.

Despite the illusory nature of the isolated word, the fact remains that in real life, where simplification is essential, we work on the basis of simple units, both of experience and of language, assuming that we can, if we wish, regard words as individual things as we regard ourselves and the things around us, choosing to ignore or forget the possibility of " the intellectual word at its zenith . . . being the totality of the relationships existing in everything ",[1] or the possibility that, as somebody has said, a baby dropping his teddy-bear out of the pram sets up eddies amongst the farthest stars. In everyday life then we assume that a word can and does exist in isolation. In poetry, however, this is not possible, because, stated in its simplest form, poetry consists of a number of words. This is a very commonplace definition of something on which so many pens have rhapsodized—and admittedly we shall have to take it further ; we might say, for instance, that it is a number of words in a particular relationship, but the important thing at this stage is the deadly dull first half of this last statement. And if poetry is a number of words, then in poetry a word cannot occur without other words, and one word alone cannot be poetry. This means that in studying the language of poetry one is bound to study a system of relationships, not a collection of self-contained units. Four lines of poetry on a page, these from *Bateau Ivre*, for instance :—

[1] Mallarmé, *Divagations*, Crise de Vers. " L'intellectuelle parole à son apogée... en tant que l'ensemble des rapports existant dans tout."

> " J'ai vu des archipels sidéraux, et des îles
> Dont les cieux délirants sont ouverts au vogueur :
> Est-ce en ces nuits sans fond que tu dors et t'exiles,
> Millions d'oiseaux d'or, ô future Vigueur ? " [1]

are not like a wall consisting of four lines of brickwork, each brick laid alongside other, each separated from other by cement--or a tiny expanse of white paper. This is not yet the time and place to say what those four lines of poetry are ; but it is important to see what they are not, because there has been a good deal of loose thinking here about individual words and poetry. Two examples follow of the kind of fallacy that can arise ; I am calling the first one the Fallacy of Dissection, the second the Fallacy of Disintegration.

By dissection I mean the process by which a poem is pulled to pieces and the pieces are then studied individually. One form of this is the process of cataloguing and classifying a writer's vocabulary, of listing neologisms and archaisms, of assessing, say, the preponderance of nouns over verbs in Rimbaud's *Illuminations*, and so on. It must be made quite plain that I do not intend to attempt this. Studies of this sort on Rimbaud and Mallarmé [2] are already in existence, and in any case I do not feel that if one is concerned with poetry one can pitch one's tent here.

The second fallacy is that of disintegration. An example of this may be seen in Bourget's statement about literature of the Symbolist period : " A style typical of decadence is one where the unity of the book decomposes, yielding place to the sentence in independence, and the sentence in its turn, yielding place to the word in independence. The writing of the present day is packed with examples which support this fruitful hypothesis." [3] This sounds as if style, language, prose, or verse were so loosely put together that

[1] I have seen starry archipelagoes, and islands
Whose delirious skies are open to the seafarer :
Is it within these bottomless nights that thou sleepest and takest thy exile,
Millions of birds of gold, o strength to come ?

[2] See Jacques Scherer, *L'Expression littéraire dans l'œuvre de Mallarmé*, Droz, Paris, 1947, for instance.

[3] Paul Bourget, *Essais de Psychologie Contemporaine*, Alphonse Lemerre, Paris, 1892, p. 25.

someone has only to cry Atishoo, Atishoo, and they all fall down. The trouble here lies partly in a fallacious simplification, assuming that language is a whole made up of the sum of its parts, and that it can be analysed into its parts; and also in the use of the word "décompose", because decomposition would seem to be restricted to organic matter, and this words are not. It is only too easy to fall into ways of thinking or speaking which imply that they are, but the result is unfortunate, as it is here, for Bourget's remark is not a "féconde hypothèse", it is nonsense.

Since analysis must fail with poetry, some other approach must be found. Mallarmé's words may be helpful here when he speaks of "the line of poetry, which from a number of syllables remakes a new and all-embracing word, a stranger in that language, almost an incantation, achieves this isolation of the word".[1] It would seem as if the approach had to be that of construction rather than destruction, seeing how the whole is made up rather than trying to break it down. But even here we meet with difficulties. There are ways in which words can be partially isolated, and Mallarmé makes liberal use of these: by punctuation, for instance—in *La Musique et les Lettres* we come upon the word "Préférablement", which is a paragraph to itself. In Rimbaud, too, the same sort of thing occurs, "Douceurs!" for example, forming a paragraph, or perhaps one should say a verse, in *Barbare* from the *Illuminations*. Words can be partially isolated by artifices of typography; Mallarmé discusses this in the *Divagations*, and practises it to the full in his poem *Un Coup de Dés* (A Throw of the Dice), where, for instance, the word "N'ABOLIRA", in capitals, stands entirely alone on its large page. Words can also be partially isolated by being surrounded by other words that differ from them in some way; this is what Lemaître is objecting to when, in an article on Verlaine, he speaks of "a great many lines such as this, which displays so uneasy a combination of a scientific term and poetic vocabulary".[2]

[1] From *Divagations*, Crise de Vers. "Le vers, qui de plusieurs vocables refait un mot total, neuf, étranger à la langue et comme incantatoire, achève cet isolement de la parole."

[2] Lemaître, *Les Contemporains*, 4e Série, p. 80.

The isolation of the word achieved in these ways is not absolute, however, and cannot be so. It is not the isolation of one individual entirely alone, the isolation of Rousseau's primitive man or of the Miller of the Dee—both legendary figures, be it noted—but the isolation of one individual in a crowd. Even the partial isolation of a word achieved in poetry consists in the *nature* of that word's relationships, not in the *absence* of relationships.

This brings us somewhere near the heart of the matter. The problem lies not in the isolated word as such, but in the nature of absolute isolation as opposed to relative isolation. It is not for nothing that both Rimbaud and Mallarmé speak of silence in connection with poetry. In *Alchimie du Verbe* from *Une Saison en Enfer*, Rimbaud says : "I wrote silences, and nights, I noted down the inexpressible. I pinned down fits of giddiness." [1] Coulon says about this : "All the resources of metre are at his disposal. . . . He prefers to stammer and stutter. He prefers . . . to write silences." [2] The tone of the passage, and particularly the dots before the last phrase which are Coulon's own, suggest that it was a perverse mistake ; but I do not think that the mistake is Rimbaud's. In Mallarmé, examples abound of the preoccupation with silence and space. The whole of his poetic work attests it, and it appears continually in his prose as well.

"All the action at one's disposal, eternally and solely, is to grasp the relationships, in the interval, rare or multiplied ; according to some interior state that one would like to extend at will, to simplify the world." [3] If this is the task of the poet, then he is faced with an impossible dilemma, because the only medium at his disposal, words, cannot be simple, cannot be simplified. Language is a system of relationships and as such it is inevitably relative—and that is not just a play upon words ; words are interdependent, relative,

[1] "J'écrivais des silences, des nuits, je notais l'inexprimable. Je fixais des vertiges."

[2] Marcel Coulon, *Le Problème de Rimbaud* : *Poète Maudit*, A. Gomès Éditeur, Nîmes, 1923, part iv, § vi.

[3] From *La Musique et les Lettres*. "Tout l'acte disponible, à jamais et seulement, reste de saisir les rapports, entre temps, rares ou multipliés ; d'après quelque état intérieur et que l'on veuille à son gré étendre, simplifier le monde."

complex. Where is simplicity in all this? Not in language, therefore outside of it; and poetry cannot go outside of language and remain poetry.

Absolute isolation is not silence of which Rimbaud and Mallarmé speak; it entails something surrounded by absolute nothingness, and that is as unattainable, humanly speaking, as absolute everythingness. Pascal says of man: "Whoso considers himself after this fashion will doubtless be terrorstruck to see himself suspended as it were, in that substance which nature has given him, between these two abysses of infinity and nothingness, equally far removed from each." So the poet is necessarily precluded from the absolute because words are relative. He could only achieve the final simplification if it were possible to have on the one hand language that effaced everything, or, on the other, language that embraced everything. Nonsense, says the rational mind; it is not possible. But though it may seem extraordinary to the rational mind, the more one looks at the work of these two poets, the more one comes to the conclusion that that was what they were working towards. Apparently the poet must do one of two things. Either he must accept the relative nature of his medium and act accordingly, as human beings do in ordinary experience, with the exception of the saint, or he must pursue the absolute, in which case he is bound to end up outside poetry. It looks as though Rimbaud and Mallarmé chose the second course but set off in opposite directions, Rimbaud in the direction of "l'infini" or infinity, Mallarmé in the direction of "le néant" or nothingness. In the case of Rimbaud, we have his own words to go on [1]:—

"Je vais dévoiler tous les mystères."

"J'ai tous les talents!"

"Je me flattai d'inventer un verbe poétique accessible, un jour ou l'autre, à tous les sens."

"Du reste, toute parole étant idée, le temps d'un langage universel viendra!"

"Cette langue sera de l'âme pour l'âme, résumant tout,

[1] Of these five quotations, the first three are from *Une Saison en Enfer*, the first and second from the section *Nuit de l'Enfer*, the third from *Alchimie du Verbe;* the fourth and fifth are from the *Lettre du Voyant*.

parfums, sons, couleurs, de la pensée accrochant à la pensée et tirant. Le poète définirait la quantité d'inconnu s'éveillant en son temps, dans l'âme universelle." [1]

One is reminded, too, of the words which Verlaine puts into the mouth of the youth in "Crimen Amoris", which Dr. Starkie, in her book on Rimbaud, applies to him: "O je serai celui-là qui sera Dieu!" (Oh I shall be he that will become God!) Mallarmé also, in his turn, bears witness to his preoccupation with nothingness as the ultimate goal.[2]

"Le silence, seul luxe après les rimes." (*Divagations.*)

"...concourant au rythme total, lequel serait le poème tu, aux blancs." (*Divagations.*)

"Évoquer, dans une ombre exprès, l'objet tu, par des mots allusifs, jamais directs, se réduisant à du silence égal, comporte tentative proche de créer." (*Divagations.*)

"À l'égal de créer: la notion d'un objet, échappant, qui fait défaut." [3] (*La Musique et les Lettres.*)

I have in each case quoted only from the critical work of these two, not from their poetry. The results of each attitude are stated in either case, for Rimbaud says in *Une Saison en Enfer*, "Ma santé fut menacée. La terreur venait" (My health was in danger. Terror set in), and Mallarmé, in

[1] I am going to unveil all mysteries.
I possess all the talents.
I flattered myself on the invention of a poetic formula accessible one day or another to all the senses.
Moreover, every word being an idea, the time of a universal language will come.
This language will be of the soul for the soul, taking in everything, scents, sounds, colours—thought hooked on to thought and pulling. The poet would define the quantity of the unknown waking, in his day, in the soul of the universe.

[2] Another poet, Lascelles Abercrombie, touches on the same point in his poem *Epitaph*, of which the last three lines run as follows:—

"I lookt for Beauty and I longed for rest,
And now I have perfection: nay, I am
Perfection. I am Nothing, I am dead."

[3] Silence, sole luxury after rhyme.
Leading to the total rhythm, which would be the poem silenced, to the white spaces on the page.
To call up, in a deliberate shadow, the un-named object, by words that are allusive, never direct, coming down to an equivalent silence—this is an attempt that borders on creation.
The equivalent of creation—the notion of an object that escapes, that is lacking.

L'Azur, speaks of " Le poète impuissant qui maudit son génie. À travers un désert stérile de Douleurs " (the impotent poet who curses his genius in a barren desert of sufferings).

" Simplifier le monde "—all Rimbaud's critics insist upon his childlike simplicity, Hackett, for instance, who says that he was " a poet who remained a child at the heart of his personality " [1]; similarly Thibaudet says of Mallarmé : " There is in him, as in Verlaine or Rimbaud, the sensibility of a child, something original, a day still wet with the waters of creation." [2] And yet in one way it seems absurd even to speak of simplicity in connection with these poets, for we are faced with an extraordinary paradox. We have the statement of the poets' task, " simplifier le monde " and we have also these two men who sought the ultimate and final simplicity, though in opposite directions. They produced what is generally regarded as some of the most intricate, difficult, and complicated poetry that has ever been written.

[1] C. A. Hackett, *Le Lyrisme de Rimbaud*, Librairie Nizet et Bastard, Paris, 1938, Introduction II, p. 23.

[2] *La Poésie de Stéphane Mallarmé* : Étude Littéraire, NRF, Gallimard, 5th edition, Bk. II, ch. iv, p. 51.

6. Relationships in General

TWO points have now emerged. First, it is useless to try to isolate units in language, so the inquiry must now move on to its second stage, words in small groups, i.e. words in relationships with other words—in fact, a relation system. Secondly, this relationship system can be looked at in a wider context, the result being the following scheme :—

Zero	Relationship system	Infinity

The interesting thing here is that this scheme does not suggest the means by which it was arrived at, namely language and poetry. It suggests mathematics. And after the initial shock, why not ? The subject matter of this study being a relationship system, one might reasonably expect assistance from similar studies in other fields (the two that at once suggest themselves are physics [1] and mathematics), and might hope to find relevant and helpful material in these different disciplines. As we shall discover, the hope is justified. The great mathematician, Henri Poincaré, makes the statement : " Mathematicians do not study objects, but relations between objects " [2] ; Bertrand Russell seconds him as follows : " A careful analysis of mathematical reasoning shows . . . that types of relations are the true subject-matter discussed " [3] ; and lastly there is Eddington : " I must still keep hammering at the question, what do we really observe ? Relativity theory has returned one answer—we only observe

[1] Cf. Sir Arthur Eddington, *New Pathways in Science*, Cambridge University Press, 1935, Epilogue, p. 312. " I think it is insufficiently realized that modern theoretical physics is very much concerned with the study of organization."

[2] Henri Poincaré, *La Science et l'Hypothèse*, Flammarion, Paris, undated, pt. i, ch. ii, p. 32.

[3] Bertrand Russell, *The Principles of Mathematics*, Cambridge University Press, 1903, ch. ii, § 27, p. 23.

relations. Quantum theory returns another answer—we only observe *probabilities*." [1]

Unfortunately, much of the scientific and mathematical world is closed to the mind which has not had that particular type of training and which may be unfitted for it by temperament and aptitude. Faced with the real technicalities one feels as the White King did :—

" The Anglo-Saxon attitudes only got more extraordinary every moment. . . .

" You alarm me ! " said the King. " I feel faint—give me a ham sandwich ! "

In selecting ideas that seem helpful I may well have distorted them inadvertently by dragging them from their context. Even in what may be a mutilated form, however, the ideas are helpful and to the point. Eddington seems to realize the possibility of this when, speaking of the child or the ordinary individual, he says : " But when we dole out to him bit by bit, in language adapted to the stage he has reached, particulars about the group structure, he recognizes that the information is an answer to his half-formed questions. And his curiosity is not satisfied until he has extracted in this way everything we can tell him about the group structure, or until we have become so unintelligible that it is useless to question us any longer." [2] That is the position exactly, and it is on that basis that we proceed.

For the moment I am going to ignore the two ends of the scheme, zero and infinity, because they raise special problems. This may mean parting company temporarily with our two chief sources of examples in this study, Mallarmé and Rimbaud, who, as I have said, were trying to pull the central relationship system the one to the one extreme, the other to the other. It is necessary, however, to stay in the middle for the present, considering the relationship system itself, with such help as other studies can give us. But there is one poet and critic who will remain in this field with us—Paul Valéry. Three statements of his will make this plain.

[1] Eddington, *The Philosophy of Physical Science*, Cambridge University Press, 1939, ch. vi, p. 89.

[2] *The Philosophy of Physical Science*, ch. x, p. 161.

" In this, he [Mallarmé]—and I told him so one day—approached the attitude of men who in algebra have examined the science of forms and the symbolic part of the art of mathematics." [1]

" But I myself could not help making a connection, which seemed to me inevitable, between the construction of an exact science and the design, plain to see in Mallarmé's case, of reconstituting the whole system of poetry by means of pure and distinct concepts, properly isolated by the delicacy and rightness of his judgment, and freed from that confusion which is caused, in minds that deal with literary matters, by the multiplicity of the functions of language." [2]

" If I am conversant only with a little of mathematics, this little has none the less played a big part (perhaps disproportionately big) in my mental life, even in the part of that life which has busied itself with poetry. . . . It is my misfortune that I scarcely ever consider literary matters in a literary light." [3] This suggests that we are on the right track.

To say that what needs looking at is (*a*) poetry and arithmetic, (*b*) poetry and algebra, sounds like nonsense, though it is not. As far as (*a*) is concerned, one might call the poets themselves to witness that poetry and numbers are in some way intimately connected.

" I lisped in numbers, for the numbers came."
(Pope, *Prologue*, *Epistle to Dr. Arbuthnot.*)

" O Goddess ! hear these tuneless numbers, wrung
By sweet enforcement and remembrance dear. . . . "
(Keats, *Ode to Psyche.*)

" Tell me not, in mournful numbers,
Life is but an empty dream. . . . "
(Longfellow, *A Psalm of Life.*)

" You shall teach us your song's new numbers
And things that we dreamed not before. . . . "
(O'Shaughnessy, *Ode.*)

[1] *Variété III*, NRF, Gallimard, Paris, 1936, p. 29.
[2] *Variété II*, NRF, Gallimard, Paris, 1930, p. 216.
[3] From a letter from Paul Valéry to the Doyen de la Faculté des Sciences de Genève and M. Rolin Wavre, quoted by the latter in *Paul Valéry*, *Essais et Témoignages Inédits*, Editions de la Baconnière, Neuchâtel, 1945, p. 157. (Letter dated 8th May, 1936.)

That numbers and poetry should have become synonymous is interesting. As for (*b*), one need only refer back to the first of the three quotations from Valéry just given to find Mallarmé and algebra mentioned in the same breath.

What is needed is help in investigating a system of relations, and evidence piles up that such help is available in the world of mathematics and logic. The fact that the relations in question here, those obtaining in language and poetry, are of an apparently specialized kind does not matter in the least. " We must think of the pattern of interweaving as abstracted altogether from the particular entities and relations that furnish the pattern. In particular, we can give an exact mathematical description of the pattern, although mathematics may be quite inappropriate to describe what we know of the nature of the entities and operations concerned in it. In this way mathematics gets a footing in knowledge which is not of a kind suggesting mathematical conceptions." That is what Eddington says (*The Philosophy of Physical Science*, p. 144), and it looks hopeful for the inquiry now in hand, as also does Wittgenstein's remark : " Where, however, we can build symbols according to a system, there this system is the logically important thing and not the single symbols." [1]

If in this chapter I labour the fact that a study of relationships in language and poetry must turn first to mathematics and science for a study of pure relations, this is merely a reflection of my own astonishment at finding the inquiry move on to what was for me wholly unfamiliar ground. This was only the prelude to greater astonishment, however, first that exactly what was needed was to be found here, secondly that nobody had ever told me about it before. It means that for the next few chapters the work will have to proceed largely with the help of quotations, for no newcomer and amateur in this field is qualified to speak about it. The quotations will serve a double purpose, however, for it may well be that this is unfamiliar ground to the reader as well, who, like myself, may need, and be glad of, a good deal of official signposting.

[1] Ludwig Wittgenstein, *Tractatus Logico-Philosophicus*, Kegan Paul, Trench, Trubner, and Co., Ltd., London, 1922, p. 147.

Two further quotations from Eddington will link all this up with the original and proper subject matter of this study. " The knowledge we can acquire is knowledge of a structure or pattern. . . . I think that the artist may partly understand what I mean." " There are two factors which, it seems to me, explain the comparative success of the mathematician. In the first place, the mathematician is the professional wielder of symbols ; he can deal with unknown quantities and even unknown operations. Clearly he is the man to help us to sift a little knowledge from a vast unknown. But the main reason why the mathematician has beaten his rivals is that we have allowed him to dictate the terms of the competition. The fate of every theory of the universe is decided by a numerical test. Does the sum come out right ? I am not sure that this mathematician understands this world of ours better than the poet and the mystic. Perhaps it is only that he is better at sums." [1] Here is a scientist putting artist, poetry, and mathematics side by side. The main thing at the moment seems to be to admit that in poetry the sums are there to be done, and to try to work out the answers to some of them. Like Alice and Humpty Dumpty, our conversation is going to be about words, sums, and the interpretation of some very obscure poetry.

[1] Eddington, *New Pathways in Science*, pp. 256 and 324.

7. Order and Disorder

" The advantage of confining attention to a definite group of abstractions is that you confine your thoughts to clear-cut definite things, with clear-cut definite relations." (Whitehead.)

" Admit that the universe is infinitely complicated, that it consists of infinite systems moving uniformly and non-uniformly relatively to one another, this only increases the difficulty of correlating observations." (Wildon Carr.)

THE mind now finds itself compelled to shift its ground, into a world of relations and of abstracts. This is new and difficult, but it is the first step towards an ordered way of thinking because it is only in the mind that an order can be established or appreciated. Only a collection in which the mind can perceive regularity of some sort can be termed ordered ; the completely irregular, which escapes the mind's efforts at perceiving regularity in it, escapes out of order into disorder. Boole, in his work on the Laws of Thought, speaks of " the ability inherent in our nature to appreciate Order, and the concurrent presumption, however founded, that the phenomena of Nature are connected by a principle of Order ".[1] It is not my concern, any more than it was Boole's, to discuss how or why we have this ability ; I am taking it for granted.

The first stage is to see how Language can be brought into some order in the mind profitable to the present purpose. This at once raises the question : What is Order ? This is to be handled gingerly or it will turn into a philosophical problem outside our terms of reference. It will perhaps be best to think of it not as an attempt to define Order but merely as the seeking of an introduction to a method of organization.

[1] George Boole, *An Investigation of the Laws of Thought*, on which are founded the Mathematical Theories of Logic and Probabilities, Walton and Maberly, London, 1854, p. 1.

One thing about this method of organization has been noted already: it must be possible to establish a principle of regularity in it, indeed in one sense the regularity *is* the system. So Wittgenstein says: "Logical research means the investigation of *all regularity*. And outside logic all is accident" (*Tractatus*, p. 173). If in the contemplation or construction of a collection a connecting principle can be established in the mind (Russell says: "Order depends upon asymmetrical relations . . . these always have two senses, as before and after, greater and less, east and west, etc." [1]), such that that mind by virtue of this principle can draw the collection into one or so construct it as to make it "hang together", so to speak—here once again is the idea that appeared in Chapter 4 of bringing unity out of diversity—with the result that the collection can be regarded as a whole, complete, accurate, and independent, then that mind will within its own boundaries have established order.

It will be noticed that there is an Either-Or in this, that the collection can be either contemplated or constructed. To this correspond two ways of producing order or rather two sides of the mind's belief in order: the first, that Order is in the mind, the second that Order is outside the mind but discoverable by it. This results in two approaches, according to which of these two is put first. Scientists appear to be divided between the two. Eddington is an example of the first when he says: "The totality of mind-made law does not impose determinism," [2] i.e. the so-called laws of nature hold only in the mind; Einstein is an example of the second when he says of the physicist: "He is astonished to notice how sublime order emerges from what appeared to be chaos. And this cannot be traced back to the workings of his own mind but is due to a quality that is inherent in the world of perception. Leibniz well expressed this quality by calling it a pre-established harmony." [3] Poetry, too, provides supporters of the one view or the other, the poet who by his poetry constructs an independent order to which

[1] *The Principles of Mathematics*, p. 227.
[2] *The Philosophy of Physical Science*, p. 180.
[3] Albert Einstein, *Preface* to Max Planck's *Where Is Science Going ?*, George Allen and Unwin, Ltd., London, 1933, p. 13.

the outer world will correspond, or the one who in his poetry expresses a new vision which conforms to another order which is independent and already in existence. The first view holds in Shakespeare's :—

> " Orpheus with his lute made trees
> And the mountain tops that freeze
> Bow themselves when he did sing. . . ."

The second holds in Milton's :—

> " O may we soon again renew that song
> And keep in tune with Heav'n. . . ."
> (*At a Solemn Musick.*)

The distinction need not necessarily be a fundamental one ; what matters is the mind's belief in and desire for Order, which may express itself in either of these two ways. In this study it seems impossible at this stage to adopt the second view and set about discovering some inherent order in the world of language. It will therefore be necessary to opt for the first of the alternatives, and attempt to construct an order in the mind in the hope that it may eventually provide a way of thinking about language that would come reasonably near to completeness, independence, and accuracy. These were quoted earlier as necessary characteristics of a collection when ordered in the mind. Boole says that they are the three necessary characteristics of premises in logic,[1] so the position is as it was in Sir Macklin's sermon in the *Bab Ballads* :—

> " That matter settled, I shall reach
> The ' Sixthly ' in my solemn tether,
> And show that what is true of each,
> Is also true of all, together.
>
> Then I shall demonstrate to you,
> According to the rules of WHATELY,
> That what is true of all, is true
> Of each, considered separately."

Unlike that discourse, however, there is no question of " To ' Twenty-firstly ' on they go ". On the contrary, we are not

[1] Op. cit., p. 153.

going on at all ; for the moment we come back to language, as the proper subject matter and the collection which is to be ordered, we are stuck at once, and the reason for this is not hard to find.

To say that we must try to construct an order in the mind means, quite simply, that we are faced with the job of constructing a logic. It is only in the realm of pure thought that both premises and finished construction can attain to completeness, independence, and accuracy. Whitehead says : " Mathematical reasoning is deductive in the sense that it is based upon definitions which, as far as the validity of the reasoning is concerned (apart from any existential import), need only the test of self-consistence " [1] ; Valéry says : " Alone, combinations that are purely abstract, purely differential, such as numerical ones, can be built up with determinate units ; note that these bear the same relation to the other possible constructions as do the regular parts of the world to those that are not regular " [2]—and both these quotations show something of what we are after. The aim apparently should be to construct a system based on regularity, purely abstract, by means of " unités déterminées ". How is language to be thought of in the abstract, so as to provide the wherewithal for such a construction ? And the answer is that it cannot be done.

After prolonged attempts to arrive at some simple way of thinking about language, about words in relations with one another, which would serve the purpose, the best I could do was this : LANGUAGE—a system fixed by virtue of a constant arbitrary connection with a variable [3] system. The first of the two systems is sound-look, the second reference. The fact that sound-look is a fixed system does not mean that it does not have its own inner organization and grouping. Some aspects of this will become plainer later on, but I am not proposing to attempt an analysis of the particular species of sound-look groupings, the French

[1] Alfred North Whitehead, *A Treatise on Universal Algebra*, with Applications, Cambridge University Press, 1898, Preface, p. vi.

[2] *Variété*, NRF, Gallimard, Paris, 1924, p. 250.

[3] I am using the term " variable " to mean something that is not fixed, not in any technical mathematical sense.

language, from which most of my examples are drawn. Such a task calls for great subtlety of mind and ear, as anyone familiar with existing studies of this sort will know, and I am certain that such analysis could be successfully undertaken only in one's native tongue. The point to be borne in mind here is that within any one manifestation of itself, such as French or English, sound-look varies very little. It is interesting that the variations, the unusual accent or the Spoonerism, are considered comic, or, like the enigma and the acrostic, belong to the world of play. Reference, too, may vary in its variability, as was seen in Chapter 4. The wholly invariable thing is the relation between the two, the fact that a word means something ; this is what makes it a word. It is this that holds language and logic, and, worse still, language and order, at arm's length, because there is a *constant* connection between sound-look and reference which makes isolation of language-units in the mind and hence abstraction, completeness, independence, and accuracy impossible ; and because the connection between sound-look and reference is *arbitrary*, which lets in chance—and there is no chance in logic. Mallarmé, in *Crise de Vers*, from the *Divagations*, speaks of " le hasard demeuré aux termes ", the residue of hazard in words. Valéry sets it out in more detail : " We know well enough that there is scarcely a single case where the relation between our ideas and the groups of sounds which call them up one by one is not wholly arbitrary or a matter of pure chance." [1] Boole, too, says the same thing : " It is clearly indifferent what particular word or token we associate with a given idea, provided that the association once made is permanent." [2] Therefore, in so far as words mean anything, they are useless to logic and mathematics ; indeed, the logician says so :

" The reader must bear in mind that the sole province of a method of inference or analysis is to determine those relations which are necessitated by the *connexion* of the terms in the original proposition. Accordingly, in estimating the completeness with which this object is effected, we have nothing whatever to do with those other relations which may

[1] *Variété III*, p. 15. [2] Op. cit., p. 26.

be suggested to our minds by the *meaning* of the terms employed, as distinct from their expressed connexion" (Boole, p. 96). But in so far as words do not mean anything, they are useless to the poet, indeed, they cease thereby to be words at all. Language belongs inevitably by the fact of reference to the world that is not the world of abstract thought, and because it does, it belongs to the realm of probabilities, or, lest that term should be misleading because of more technical uses of it, to the realm of uncertainty and accident, where there is disorder as well as order.

Whether this property of language, the connection with something that cannot be reduced to logic, is regarded as good or bad will depend on the point of view adopted. If abstract thought is considered to be the be-all and end-all of life, then the property is bad, and indeed there is a good deal of complaining among certain scientific writers on this point. But such an attitude carries strange implications with it. There are two phrases in Thibaudet's work on Mallarmé (pp. 115 and 108) which illustrate this well when set side by side :—

"The necessity of words meaning something—that is . . . the stumbling block."

"That which in some obscure way constitutes a permanent scandal to any idealist—the fact of existence."

The purer the abstraction, the nearer it approaches to nothingness. There will be more to say about this shortly, but, meanwhile, objections to "signification" should be seen in their real light, as objections to "existence". This is the negative side. On the positive side, which objects neither to language nor life, I believe one might set the Christian doctrine of the Word made flesh.

The connection between word and reference creates grave difficulties for the student, because it means that there is an unbreakable link between the subject-matter of study and the complexity of life itself, of the whole of experience. Whitehead and Russell, in the Introduction to their *Principia Mathematica*, say : "The grammatical structure of language is adapted to a wide variety of uses. Thus, it possesses no unique simplicity in representing the few simple, though highly abstract, processes and ideas arising in the deductive trains of reasoning employed here. In fact, the very abstract simplicity of the ideas of this work defeats language. Language can represent concrete ideas more easily. The proposition ' a whale is big ' represents language at its best, giving terse expression to a complicated fact ; while the true analysis of ' one is a number ' leads, in language, to an intolerable prolixity." [1]

Any way of thinking about language will therefore have to rule out from the start any hope of simplification. It will have from the beginning to handle as its data a double relationship-system. This is an extraordinary and alarming prospect for a mind unaccustomed to dealing with any relationship systems whatever, but it is unavoidable. Unable to have the fun (or the illusion) of complicated thinking with simple subject matter, we shall have to content ourselves with simple thinking about complicated subject matter. Of the other two possibilities, the ideal—simple thought with simple units—is ruled out by the indefinitely unlimited nature of my subject matter, complex thought with complex material by the definitely limited nature of my head. Whatever happens, we must hold on to the order in the mind. With this in view, we will take refuge in a diagram (Fig. 1).

Perfect Order	Order	Probable Order	Probable Disorder	Disorder	Perfect Disorder
	←Logic—				
	←—— Num	ber———			
		←—— Lang	uage——→		
			——— D	ream ——→	
				— Nightmare →	

Fig. 1

[1] *Principia Mathematica*, Cambridge University Press, 1910, p. 2.

One thing needs to be said about this diagram here and now—it is nothing more than a way I have adopted of looking at things. It is not a classification of experience, nor a map of the mind. It does bear one resemblance to a map, however, or rather to Mercator's Projection, because it would be better thought of as joining up at the two ends, i.e. as round rather than flat.[1]

I propose to talk about the two extremes first and so work in towards the middle.

The two extremes are left a blank because they are plainly beyond the reach of a human mind. Perfect order, the " final synthesis " as I called it earlier, and perfect disorder, in its own way complete and final also, are not just the last terms in a progression [2]; they are something different, and constitute their own order of being, from which we are excluded. Valéry maintains that we cannot even conceive of them : " If we must have some idea of a nothingness, the idea of nothing is nothing ; or rather it is already something : it is a make-believe of the mind which creates for itself a farce of silence and total darkness, in which I know perfectly well that I am hidden, ready for the act of creation, by a mere relaxation of my attention " [3]; and again : " We obscurely imagine that *everything* is *something*, and so we imagine *something* and call it *everything*. . . . Such is the primitive and, as it were, the childish form of our notion of the universe." [4] Pascal says exactly the same thing : " Let us realize our scope ; we are something and are not everything ; the being that we have robs us of the knowledge of first principles, which spring from the void ; and the littleness of the being that we have hides from us the sight of infinity." Therefore, whatever one may say about these different orders of being will be nonsense. But this does not mean that the nonsense is useless ; indeed, it

[1] For the idea that the two extremes come to one and the same thing, cf. Dorothy Margaret Eastwood, *The Revival of Pascal*, A Study of his Relation to Modern French Thought, Clarendon Press, Oxford, 1936, ch. iii, p. 34. " . . . the character of form without content which is the first step towards formlessness."

[2] Cf. Russell, *The Principles of Mathematics*, ch. xxii, where he says that the problem of zero bears no relation to the problem of the infinitesimal.

[3] *Variété*, p. 130.

[4] Ibid., p. 132.

may be interesting and helpful—possibly even inevitable. Poe says about this: "The human brain has obviously a leaning to the '*Infinite*', and fondles the phantom of the idea. It seems to long with a passionate fervour for this impossible conception, with the hope of intellectually believing it when conceived. What is general among the whole race of man, of course no individual of that race can be warranted in considering abnormal." [1] These are the vanishing points of thought,[2] and with that other creature which knew all about vanishing, the Cheshire Cat, I would say: "We're all mad here. I'm mad. You're mad."

The statement that perfect order constitutes a vanishing point of some kind may sound a fanciful one, but it seems as if there is some part of the mind that believes it to be true. Surely this is what lies at the back of such phrases as "too good to live", of the many stories of saints being rapt away to Heaven, of St. John's statement, twice repeated: "No man hath seen God at any time." There is an interesting example of this sort of thinking in H. V. Morton's *In Search of England*; he says of Exeter Cathedral: "It is like a problem in mathematics set to music. It is almost too perfect! At one moment it seems that the whole fragment might fly up to heaven or dissolve in cold formal music. The thing that keeps Exeter Cathedral firmly rooted to earth is the organ. . . . This is Exeter's anchor of ugliness." It is an idea that may suggest itself quite normally to any mind, and that is all that I am concerned with at the moment: Perfect Order is Zero.

The same thing holds good with total disorder, "le désordre à l'état parfait." [3] This sounds like a contradiction in terms, but Valéry explains elsewhere what may be understood by the phrase: "A really fundamental confusion ought to be an infinite confusion. But then we could not extract the world from it, and the very perfection of the chaos would forbid us for ever to make use of it." [4] This

[1] From Poe's Essay *Eureka*.

[2] Cf. Boole, op. cit., ch. iii, § 13, p. 47. "In fact, Nothing and Universe are the two limits of class extension, for they are the limits of the possible interpretations of general names, none of which can relate to fewer individuals than are comprised in Nothing, or to more than are comprised in the Universe."

[3] Valéry, *Variété*, p. 18.

[4] Ibid., p. 131.

perfection, too, the antithesis of perfect order, comes to the same thing in the end as far as the human mind is concerned, since it also constitutes a vanishing point for the mind. Examples may be found in such words as " And the earth was without form, and void ; and darkness was upon the face of the deep " from Genesis ; in

> " The cloud-capp'd towers, the gorgeous palaces,
> The solemn temples, the great globe itself,
> Yea, all which it inherit, shall dissolve,
> And, like this insubstantial pageant faded,
> Leave not a rack behind."
>
> (From *The Tempest.*)

in Milton's phrase " the reign of Chaos and old Night ", from *Paradise Lost*, and in all the apocalyptic visions of the end of the world, " And I beheld when he had opened the sixth seal, and, lo, there was a great earthquake ; and the sun became black as sackcloth of hair, and the moon became as blood ;

And the stars of heaven fell unto the earth, even as a fig tree casteth her untimely figs, when she is shaken of a mighty wind.

And the heaven departed as a scroll when it is rolled together ; and every mountain and island were moved out of their places.

* * *

. . . the earth and the heaven fled away ; and there was found no place for them." (Revelation.)

We have already remarked, with Poe, that these two other orders of being have a fascination for the mind ; one is tempted to say a fatal fascination—for the mind is aware, too, of a certain sense of danger, of some deep-rooted conviction that to meddle with either is exceedingly dangerous. Primitive people will deliberately endow anything they make or do or possess with imperfection, and we call it superstition. But here are two remarks of Valéry, surely the last person whom one could call either primitive or superstitious, which bear out this view : " two dangers ceaselessly threaten the world : order and disorder " [1] ; " Extreme order, which is automatism, would be its ruin ; extreme disorder would lead it [human thought] even more rapidly towards the abyss." [2] The danger sensed here, and the fear that results, may be explained, in part at any rate, by something which I said earlier ; these two orders constitute *a vanishing point for the mind*—and in the ambiguity of that phrase lies the fear. At the point of contact with absolute order or absolute disorder, what vanishes—the world or the mind ? To the mind considering this question, it seems that if it were capable of " taking in " (and I use the phrase deliberately) absolute nothingness or absolute everythingness, one of two things would happen. Either everything else would vanish, leaving the mind alone, or the mind would vanish. Whether it be an alternative or one and the same thing, it is a possibility that the mind dare not contemplate. " I am my world," as Wittgenstein says (*Tractatus*, p. 151).

It is interesting to see how this links up with two things mentioned earlier. First, this question of an alternative that may not prove to be one seems to have connections with the point, raised at the beginning of this chapter, that there might be two ways of looking at order, as internal or external to the mind. Secondly, this talk about vanishing points bears on the connection between life and language via reference. Should the vanishing point be reached, the mind's existence and identity are affected. There are strange passages in Mallarmé which suggest that he held the view that the mind is only sure it exists by virtue of language.

" Sait-on ce que c'est qu'écrire ? une ancienne et très vague mais jalouse pratique, dont gît le sens au mystère du cœur.

Qui l'accomplit, intégralement, se retranche.

Autant, par ouï dire, que rien existe et soi, spécialement, au reflet de la divinité éparse : c'est, ce jeu insensé d'écrire, s'arroger, en vertu d'un doute — la goutte d'encre apparentée à la nuit sublime — quelque devoir de tout recréer, avec des réminiscences, pour avérer qu'on est bien

[1] *Variété*, p. 20. [2] Ibid., p. 40.

là où l'on doit être (parce que, permettez-moi d'exprimer cette appréhension, demeure une incertitude)." [1]

"...produire sur beaucoup un mouvement qui te donne en retour l'émoi que tu en fus le principe, donc existes : dont aucun ne se croit, au préalable, sûr "... [2]

We can take the matter no farther for the moment. It is at bottom the question propounded at the end of *Alice Through the Looking Glass* ; was it the Red king's dream or our dream ? But in either case it was a *dream*—nonsense, in fact, as I said at the beginning.

Returning to the diagram, we move further in and come to the respective domains of logic and mathematics, on the one hand, and nightmare and dream on the other. A good deal has already been said about the first of these groups, so we can pass over this fairly summarily here. It would have been easier to make logic and number coextensive, but there are two reasons for not doing so : (*a*) expert witnesses make it plain that symbolic logic and number, though related, are separate [3] ; (*b*) logic, used as it is here in the narrowest sense of the word, must end where probability begins. Number, which is also in this field, belongs to the field of logic, but also to that of probabilities, and overlaps with language to a certain extent. At the other end of the diagram are the fields of nightmare and dream. Like number, the latter overlaps into the field of probability and language.

In the middle, embracing the realm of the probable, the

[1] From *Villiers de l'Isle-Adam.*

Is it known what writing is? An ancient and very vague but jealous practice, whose sense lies in the mystery of the heart. Whoever achieves it wholly is digging himself in. Inasmuch as, by hearsay, nothing exists, oneself in particular, in the reflection of the scattered divinity : this senseless game of writing is to take upon oneself, in virtue of a doubt—the drop of ink being related to the sublime night—some duty of recreating everything, with reminiscences, to vouch for one's really being there where one ought to be (because, if I may be permitted to express the apprehension, an uncertainty persists.)

[2] From *Divagations*, Quant au Livre.

. . . to produce upon many a movement which in turn gives you the feeling that you were the prime mover, therefore exist : of which no one in the first place is certain.

[3] Cf. Whitehead, *Universal Algebra*, Preface, p. viii. "Such algebras are mathematical sciences, which are not essentially concerned with number or quantity," and Book I, ch. i, p. 11. "But the laws of Algebra, though suggested by Arithmetic, do not depend on it."

debatable ground between order and disorder, there is language. It can never by its own nature attain to order, i.e. to logic, or to disorder, i.e. to nightmare. As we have already seen, it has, by virtue of the fact of reference or meaning, to remain in the middle.

The dotted line down the middle of the diagram is a hypothetical central stage in language where the stresses and strains between order and disorder meet. Directed thought, as we have already seen, tries through language to pull as much as possible of its material, experience, out of probable disorder into probable order. " Prose always presupposes the universe of experience and of action—a universe in which—or *because of which*—our perceptions and actions or emotions have finally to respond or correspond with one another in one way and one only—*uniformly*." [1] (One needs perhaps to be reminded that it cannot do more than attain *probable* order, because, as we have seen, logic excludes " real content ". Boole says of mind-made laws of nature : " They are in all cases, and in the strictest sense of the term, *probable* conclusions, approaching, indeed, ever and ever nearer to certainty, as they receive more and more of the confirmation of experience. But of the character of probability, in the strict and proper sense of that term, they are never wholly divested.") [2]

" Mais la vérité et la vie sont désordre," [3] truth and life are disorder. Counteracting the force that pulls towards order in the mind, there is an equally strong pull the other way, towards disorder. Here the dream comes into its own, the process of redressing the balance coming to our attention chiefly when we are asleep. It is not confined to sleep, however, and I am using the word " dream " in a wide sense. Diderot speaks of " La folie, le rêve, le décousu de la conversation ", the element of madness, dream, incoherence, in conversation [4] ; Valéry speaks of thought as " le rêve d'un dormeur éveillé ",[5] the dream of a waking

[1] Valéry, *Variété III*, p. 66.
[2] Op. cit., ch. 1, p. 4.
[3] Valéry, *Variété II*, p. 79.
[4] Quoted by J.-J. Mayoux, *Diderot and the Technique of Modern Literature*, Modern Language Review No. XXXI, October, 1936, p. 524.
[5] *Variété*, p. 225.

sleeper, and of "that familiar chaos that the common run of people call *thought*, unaware that its *natural* conditions are no less fortuitous, and no less futile, than the conditions of a charade." [1] Nightmare, as distinct from dream, is the process achieved, static disorder. Valéry gives an excellent definition of it: "Nightmare knits up into an all-powerful drama a certain diversity of independent sensations that works upon us in sleep. . . . There results from it an original creation, something absurd, incompatible with the ordinary course of life, all-powerful and all-terrifying, *having within itself no principle that might bring about its end, no issue, no limit*. . . . The dreamer's mind resembles a system upon which the exterior forces cancel out or do not act, and in which the interior motions can produce neither displacement of the centre nor rotation." [2]

Because it is the function of directed thinking to pull in the direction of order, there is a tendency to regard order as good and disorder as bad, but this is far too simple a point of view. Whitehead seems much nearer the mark when he says: "There is no reason to hold that confusion is less fundamental than is order." [3] Both principles, of order and disorder, exist in the mind; and they meet in the field of probabilities, which is also the field of language. Now language in everyday life may move with thought in one direction or the other; it may become wholly subservient to practical considerations—"To be understood—to understand—these are the boundaries between which this language that is practical, that is to say abstract, increasingly encloses itself", [4] this being the tendency towards number and abstraction; or it may take on the character of undirected thought and lapse into random discontinuity. But there is another way of using language which may be conceived as holding the balance between order and disorder, not by fixation but by movement, by bringing order out of disorder and disorder out of order, transposing sense and nonsense in a perpetual process: Poetry, which holds out a hand either way to number and dream, which moves where

[1] Ibid., p. 67.
[2] *Variété II*, pp. 251, 252, 266.
[3] *Modes of Thought*, Cambridge University Press, 1938, p. 70.
[4] Valéry, *Variété III*, p. 26.

language moves (—and "*The limits of my language* are the limits of my world",[1]) but whose place is on that hypothetical line where order and disorder meet in the field of probabilities. "The Poet, without being aware of it, moves in an order of *possible* relationships and transformations." [2] Here is the final and noblest game of skill and hazard, the wager against odds, number, and calculation versus chance and probability—and the poet says: "Toute Pensée émet un Coup de Dés," every thought casts a throw of the dice, that magnificent image which embodies all that has been discussed here. If we are so far right, poetry is the perpetual process of what Poe calls "reciprocity of adaptation". "Alors, entre l'ordre et le désordre règne un instant délicieux," [3] the exquisite and brief moment between order and disorder.

[1] Wittgenstein, op. cit., p. 149.
[2] Valéry, *Variété III*, p. 49.
[3] Valéry, *Variété II*, p. 61.

8. Statics and Dynamics of Language and Poetry

THE attempt to arrive at a way of thinking about words in groups, and the resulting relationships, has already led to the introduction of such terms as fixation and movement, fields where two contending forces are at work, equilibrium between the two. In Chapters 3 and 4 the notions of equilibrium and resistance in the individual word have occurred. Set all these notions together, and the result is that for the second time in this study it becomes necessary to seek assistance in an apparently alien field ; for the notions set out above are the fundamental ones of mechanics, of statics and dynamics. And once again this new field of exploration proves helpful.

The connection may seem a doubtful one at the start, because the word " mechanics " suggests to the layman something very concrete, and it is plain that to attempt any kind of close analogy between a piece of machinery and a piece of poetry would be foolishness. The word " mechanism " is less definite in its associations than " mechanics ", but that is probably only a question of loose usage. It is very easy to talk about " the mechanism of language " or " the mechanism of poetry " without the phrase being anything other than a covering for lack of thought. The only way in which we can avoid this emptiness, this shadow-world of metaphor, will be to take the comparison seriously. A writer on physics has said : " Since the word is used in this way, we have every right to expect that the mechanism of chemical action has something in common with the mechanism of a lathe, for example. This is the way in which the problems now selected for discussion are to be approached. What there is to be said here of importance is so because it does not involve detailed technical knowledge of particular machines or particular processes. We are concerned with the logical essence of mechanism." [1]

The hope for enlightenment here depends on the existence of a sufficient body of abstract and unapplied theory in mechanics. This hope is justified, and so the matter becomes comparatively straightforward. It is no longer a question of an analogy between two totally different things, the comparison of which may turn out to be illuminating, nor of a vague metaphor. The two things have become one and the same, for on the level of abstraction all things meet.

It has already been indicated how, as soon as one begins to think about words in groups, one has to think of them at the abstract level, as systems of relations. That the same thing holds good of mechanics becomes evident from even a slight study of the subject. There are ample quotations to prove such a contention : "Purely mechanical phenomena, accordingly, are abstractions, made, either intentionally or from necessity, for facilitating our comprehension of things " [2] ; " In the process of formulation the Science [i.e. of Mechanics] acquires the character of an abstract logical theory, in which all that is assumed is suggested by experience, all that is found is proved by reasoning. The test of the validity of a theory of this kind is its consistency with itself." [3] " The laws which are to be imposed on these ideal representations [i.e. of dynamics] are in the first instance largely at our choice, since we are dealing now with mental objects " [4] ; " It should be clear that the laws of mechanics are the laws of our method of representing mechanical phenomena, and that since we actually choose a method of representation when we describe the world, it cannot be that the laws of our method say anything about the world " [5] ; lastly, two statements by

[1] W. H. Watson, *On Understanding Physics*, Cambridge University Press, 1938, ch. iv, p. 67.

[2] Ernst Mach, *The Science of Mechanics* : A Critical and Historical Exposition of its Principles. Translated from the 2nd German Edition by Thomas J. McCormack, The Open Court Publishing Co., Chicago, 1893, ch. v, p. 495.

[3] A. E. H. Love, *Theoretical Mechanics* : An Introductory Treatise on the Principles of Dynamics, 3rd edition, Cambridge University Press, 1921, Introduction, p. 1.

[4] Horace Lamb, *Dynamics*, Cambridge University Press, 1914. Appendix, p. 340.

[5] Watson, op. cit., ch. iii, p. 52.

Hertz, the first a simple statement confirming this particular point, the second coming much nearer home: "To investigate in detail the connections of definite material systems is not the business of mechanics," [1] and then: "In the text we take the natural precaution of expressly limiting the range of our mechanics to inanimate nature; how far its laws extend beyond this we leave as quite an open question. . . . Perhaps such considerations will be regarded as out of place here. It is not usual to treat of them in the elements of the customary representation of mechanics." [2] The scientist, wise man, leaves well alone; we, faced with problems of force and equilibrium in poetry, cannot. These quotations, however, will at least show that this is not some fantastical connection of my own contriving, but that at this level poetry and mechanics *are* in relation—in short, that the relation does not need to be invented but investigated.

As seems to be the general case with science, mechanics has the great advantage over poetry that its material can be reduced to abstract simplicity, and so becomes manageable and certain in the mind. In mechanics, the general notions of force and equilibrium, so long as they remain unapplied, are entirely under control. "It is not as something independent of us and apart from us that force now makes its appearance, but as a mathematical aid whose properties are entirely in our power." [3] "When, however, we occupy ourselves with cases of equilibrium, we are concerned simply with a *schematic* reproduction in thought of the mechanical facts." [4] These distinct forces act upon systems of distinct units or points: fully known action on a system of fully known units. The contrast with any study of language is obvious; here the simpler forms of approach are not possible. One way of looking at the subject matter, however, seems promising; this is to consider what I shall call open and closed systems in the mind, postulating two equal and opposing forces, one towards order, the other towards disorder.

[1] Heinrich Hertz, *The Principles of Mechanics* presented in a New Form, translated by D. E. Jones and J. T. Walley, Macmillan and Co. Ltd., London, 1899, Introduction, p. 27.

[2] Ibid., p. 38. [3] Hertz, op. cit., p. 28. [4] Mach, op, cit., ch. iii, p. 259.

Planck divides forces into internal and external, as indeed mechanics does in general. " We may divide all active forces into *internal* and *external* forces. Internal forces are all those which arise from points of the system, external forces are all those which arise from points outside the system. The question as to whether a certain force on which we fix our attention is an internal or an external force may accordingly be decided only when we have made our choice of the system of points, this choice being quite arbitrary at the outset. In this way we can convert every internal force into an external force by excluding the point at which it arises from the system, and conversely." [1] Mechanics can choose where forces are to be regarded as internal and where as external ; language cannot. One might start by thinking that the two forces, order and disorder, with which we are dealing here are in the mind, and hence external to words. But words are in the mind as well, and the distinction will not work. Language then is continually subject to internal and external forces ; this fits in with its being coextensive with the field of probability. Poetry is a particular way of organizing language, and it seems possible that the aim of poetry, " an operation which is long, difficult, delicate, which demands the most diverse qualities of mind, and which is never fully accomplished, as indeed it is never strictly possible," [2] is to turn language from an open system into a closed one. Valéry says : " In essence the world of the poem is closed and self-sufficient, being the pure system of the ornaments and the chances of language." [3]

The next question is : what may be considered as constituting an open and a closed system ? Both depend on force, internal and external. A closed system is not one where no force, either internal or external, is active, but where, as I take it, internal force is sufficient to balance external force and so to keep it external to the system. In an open system, this balance cannot be maintained, and consequently the system is liable to constant and arbitrary

[1] Max Planck, *General Mechanics*, being vol. i of " Introduction to Theoretical Physics ", translated by Henry L. Brose, Macmillan and Co., Ltd., London, 1933, pt. ii, ch. ii, p. 199.

[2] Valéry, *Variété*, p. 170.

[3] *Variété*, p. 159.

disturbance by external force. Quite simply, it is a matter of equilibrium between two equal and opposing forces.

It is necessary to emphasize once again that whatever may be said here comes itself under the heading of a mental system, a way of looking at things, nothing more. One may speak of forces, equilibrium, resistance in language and poetry ; but it is only the mind that senses these opposing forces, that is aware of a sensation of stability or instability, that experiences resistance in certain connections. Words, isolated or grouped together, have no force in themselves ; they do not move about, balance, or topple, nor do they exercise resistance—the notion is as foolish and delightful as if the thinker whose ideas got stuck called on the words to get out and push. This may sound ridiculously obvious. " Lack of clearness on this matter . . . comes from muddling the distinction between idea and thing." [1] The ridiculous thing, however, is not the obviousness of the muddle but the ease with which it is made.

The mind has a choice of systems within which it can work, and the ones we are concerned with are those set out in Fig. 1. Of these five systems, logic, number, language, dream, nightmare, the two extremes are closed systems. The middle one, language, is open. The other two, number and dream, belong to both types, i.e. they are in part open in so far as they include language, and in part closed in so far as they include logic and nightmare respectively. To have systems which are in this half-and-half state seems slightly anomalous, as was the position of Edward Lear's character :

> " There was an Old Man, who supposed
> That the street door was partially closed ;
> But some very large rats
> Ate his coats and his hats
> While that futile old gentleman dozed."

However, the supposition seems to be unavoidable.

I am taking the two contending forces to be constant in all five systems, as indeed they must be if they are held to be constant in the mind, since these systems are only ways in which the mind may work. Such equilibrium as is achieved

[1] Watson, op. cit., ch. ii, p. 27.

will therefore be the result of a balance of forces, not of the absence of forces. The distinction is made plain by Poinsot : " Equilibrium may be distinguished from rest, in that, in the second case, the body is not solicited by any force, whereas, in the other case, it is solicited by forces which annul one another. This distinction, which is meaningless in conditions of full rigour, makes itself felt in the examples of equilibrium produced by nature : scarcely a single body is precisely in equilibrium ; and even when it appears to be so to us, there exists none the less between the soliciting forces a perpetual struggle." [1] Add to this one further statement : " Absolute zero we know no more than we know absolute rest," [2] and it seems to follow that absolute rest, the equilibrium which results from the absence of forces, belongs in the realm of Absolute Order or Absolute Disorder. It is interesting that the poets themselves have identified it with death, in the Lotos Eaters, for instance, where voices sound " as voices from the grave ", or in Goethe's *Faust*. This is the Enchanted Ground where pilgrims must not tarry, " lest sleeping we never awake more."

It is not because they are unassailed by forces that the two systems are closed, but because the two forces are balanced the one against the other. The equilibrium in the case of each system is achieved by making one of the two forces internal, and letting it counteract the other. In the case of logic, the system includes all that is order and excludes all that is disorder. " The primary control of the concepts of mathematics is that contradiction should not be involved." [3] Nightmare works in reverse, including all that is disorder and excluding all that is order. In the one system there is the certainty of the expected, in the other the certainty of the unexpected, but in neither system is there any room for probability or uncertainty. Thus, equilibrium is achieved between internal force and external

[1] L. Poinsot, *Éléments de Statique*, suivis de quatre mémoires, 10e édition, Mallet-Bachelier, Paris, 1861, pp. 3–4.

[2] Alfred Daniell, *A Text Book of the Principles of Physics*, the Macmillan Co., New York, 1911, ch. vi, p. 145.

[3] P. W. Bridgman, *The Nature of Physical Theory*, Princeton University Press, 1936, p. 52.

force ; "it is plain that two equal and contrary forces applied to the same point are in equilibrium." [1]

The results of this are interesting. Both logic and nightmare are, as we have seen, outside the field of probability, so that nonsense cannot accidentally break into logic nor sense into nightmare. The equilibrium that is achieved is stable, or static. Mechanics says of this state : "A position of stable equilibrium is a position in which the potential energy is a minimum." [2] A poet says of it : "Whatever it may be, a thought that has become static assumes the characteristics of a hypnosis and becomes, in the language of logic, an idol ; in the field of poetic construction, an unfruitful monotony." [3] The fact that they are both closed systems, and the only two closed systems of the mind, seems to give them some strange affinity.

In actual experience, the mind does not (possibly cannot) remain for long in either of these two closed systems. They are, however, the only two mental systems which possess stable equilibrium, and we have already seen how urgently the mind seeks after such in its ordinary day-to-day experience ; it is ironic that the two fields where stable balance is to be found exclude life and experience, and hence are useless from this point of view.

The result is that the mind has to make do with other less certain systems. Language is the least certain of all, and hence the great importance of number and dream can be understood. Each has a double character, belonging partly to a field of certainty, partly to one of uncertainty, a system partly closed and partly open. Number belongs partly to language and partly to logic ; dream belongs partly to language and partly to nightmare. This is their great importance—they offer the appearance of an escape from uncertainty, or of a transmutation of uncertainty into certainty. In language itself, as we have seen, there is no escape from the field of uncertainty and probability, because of the arbitrary constant of meaning in words. Stable equilibrium is not possible in this hazardous realm.

[1] Poinsot, op. cit., p. 9.
[2] A. Wilmer Duff, Editor, *A Text Book of Physics*, 4th edition, J. and A. Churchill, London, 1916, p. 77.
[3] Valéry, *Variété*, p. 226.

In language, none the less, the mind may see two possibilities of security, two ways of annulling the forces ; one would be to get it all into the field of number, the other to get it all into the field of dream, as if it were necessary to concentrate upon the one force or the other, regarding sense and nonsense as mutually exclusive. The first is the turn of mind which says : " There is no translation of nonsense into sense. In making sense therefore must lie the essence of language," [1] or again : " There is a place for healthy intolerance of nonsense in all serious occupations " [2] ; but intolerance of nonsense is no more healthy than intolerance of sense, which is the characteristic of the second way of thinking, and may be seen in such things as surrealism.

It is now becoming possible to see more clearly the nature of the equilibrium which poetry may have to offer, not by trying to take up a position in one camp or the other but by effecting a transposition between the forces at work in the two, not fixation but dance. This is unstable equilibrium, but " a position of unstable equilibrium is a position in which the potential energy is a maximum ".[3]

Two other things seem to share with poetry this power of transposing sense and nonsense. The one is laughter, which delights in the union of sequence and inconsequence. The other is religion, which also suggests a power that delights equally in ordering disorder and disordering order,

> " Who hath measured the waters in the hollow of his hand, and meted out heaven with the span . . . that turneth wise men backward, and maketh their knowledge foolish."
>
> (Isaiah xl, 12, and xliv, 25.)

Only this union of sense and nonsense, order and disorder, as it appears in poetry, however, is our concern ; and the next step will be to consider more closely the relations between language, number, and dream.

[1] Watson, op. cit., ch. i, p. 12.
[2] Watson, op. cit., ch. i, p. 20.
[3] Duff, op. cit., loc. cit. For discussion of equilibrium as a basic æsthetic principle, see C. K. Ogden, I. A. Richards, James Wood, *The Foundations of Aesthetics*, George Allen and Unwin, Ltd., London, 1922.

9. Number and Dream

" Welche Zusammenstellung ! Die Zahl Zehn soll also auf eine Stufe mit Hallucinationen stehen ! " (Frege.)

(*Lit.*—Fancy putting these side by side ! So the number 10 is to be put on the same level as hallucinations !)

NUMBER and Dream, taken individually, are among the most familiar features of the life of any mind. From this, partly, springs their importance here, for if, in fact, that particular manipulation of language called poetry does make use of both in some way, it is entering upon no strange land in so doing. The very familiarity of each, however, may impede comprehension of its nature. Like the wireless, it is possible to switch on either without the slightest consideration, let alone understanding, of its workings. So some investigation of the workings of each may be useful before considering the connections of these two systems with language and poetry.

By " Number " here is meant the system of natural numbers, 0, 1, 2, 3, and so on. By " Dream " is meant night and day dream, what Jung calls " phantastic " or " undirected " thinking.[1] Psychologists appear to agree on the impossibility of differentiating between the sleeping and the waking mind in this connection.[2]

[1] Dr. C. G. Jung, *Psychology of the Unconscious* : A Study of the Transformations and Symbolisms of the Libido. A Contribution to the History of the Evolution of Thought. Translated by Beatrice M. Hinkle. Kegan Paul, Trench, Trubner, and Co., Ltd., London, 1921, passim.

[2] Cf. Sigmund Freud, *The Interpretation of Dreams*, translated A. A. Brill, George Allen and Unwin, Ltd., London, 1913, ch. vi, p. 393. " A more thorough examination of these day phantasies shows with what good reason the same name has been given to these formations as to the products of our nocturnal thought—dreams. They possess an essential part of their properties in common with nocturnal dreams."

Dr. Heinrich Spitta, *Die Schlaf- und Traumzustände der Menschlichen Seele* : mit besonderer Berücksichtigung ihres Verhältnisses zu den psychischen Alienationen, 2nd edit., Franz Fues, Tübingen, 1882, ch. iv, p. 117. " As we have seen, sleep and waking are not complements and opposites, they are closely interrelated—they are both subject to precisely the same laws."

The juxtaposition of Number and Dream, the lumping of them together, may at first sight seem strange, and some explanation may be needed, if only to quiet the indignant ghost whose words are quoted at the head of the chapter. The explanation is implicit in Fig. 1 ; it is simply that each is to be considered as a valid mental system in itself, valid according to its own organization, a consistent whole. In the case of Number, this probably will not be challenged ; two mathematicians shall speak for it : " The chain of these numbers [positive integers] forms in itself an exceedingly useful instrument for the human mind " [1] ; " The whole numbers . . . take a perfectly determined place in our understanding, are clearly distinguished from all other constituents of our thought, stand in definite relations to them, and thus modify, in a definite way, the substance of the mind." [2] To say the same thing of Dream may seem a more doubtful proceeding ; but here Freud may be cited, who says of Dream : " It is a psychic phenomenon of full value." [3] Greenwood also expresses the opinion that dreams " should be studied as rendering indications of mental processes, and above all of mental power. It is already clear enough that there is no reason why the play of mental faculty in dreams should be more unworthy of serious observation than the play and product of will-directed thought." [4]

Once again it is structure that is important rather than the elements of which that structure is made. What matters is the nature of a system. Boole defines it in terms of a self-contained aggregate of particular relations,[5] Max Black as " the relations between the forms of complex symbols ".[6] From either of these two points of view it is clear that

[1] Richard Dedekind, *Essays on the Theory of Numbers*, translated by Wooster Woodruff Beman, Open Court Publishing Co., Chicago, 1909, p. 4.

[2] Georg Cantor, *Contributions to the Founding of the Theory of Transfinite Numbers*, translated and with Introduction by Philip E. B. Jourdain, Open Court Publishing Co., Chicago and London, 1915, p. 67.

[3] Freud, op. cit., ch. 3, p. 103.

[4] Frederick Greenwood, *Imagination in Dreams and their Study*, John Lane, London, 1894, p. 147.

[5] Op. cit., ch. xxii, p. 399.

[6] *The Nature of Mathematics* : A Critical Survey, Kegan Paul, Trench, Trubner, and Co., Ltd., London, 1933, p. 24.

Dream may be regarded as a system of mental relationships, and hence can be compared with Number at this level.

What must be avoided is the reference of either system to experience, for it is in this that the apparent gulf between Number and Dream lies. It is easy enough to see the gulf, to say that Number makes sense and Dream nonsense of life. Jeans says on the first point : " We can then acquire real knowledge of the external world of physics, but this must always consist of ratios, or in other words, of numbers." [1] As for the statement that Dream makes nonsense of life, anyone can verify this by direct experience. Jung says on phantasy : " It is not to be taken seriously as such. . . . If we take it, however, as important *per se*, then the thing is not understandable, and makes one despair of the efficiency of the mind." [2] But that is just exactly what is wanted here—the Dream *is* to be taken seriously as such, not to be regarded as a lunatic distortion of reality nor as a cryptogram to be unravelled in terms of subconscious emotion and memory. Both these ways of looking at the Dream are legitimate in their own sphere, but they both relate it to experience, and that is an irrelevance here. Number and Dream can stand side by side only when regarded as relation systems in the mind.

One further argument against setting them side by side is that they are opposites, mutually exclusive.[3] It is a fact of experience that if one is working with numbers, i.e. doing arithmetic, one cannot dream ; if one is dreaming, one cannot do arithmetic. Valéry says about systems of the mind : " Each of these figures can be compared with a dream ; each is a complete and closed system, which is sufficient to cover completely or to mask the multiplicity of reality. The vision of one of these systems excludes that of the others." [4] This is certainly true of the two closed systems mentioned earlier, logic and nightmare—between which and

[1] Sir James Jeans, *Physics and Philosophy*, Cambridge University Press, 1942, ch. i, p. 8.

[2] Op. cit., ch. i, p. 20.

[3] Christopher Caudwell disagrees with this in his book *Illusion and Reality*, A Study of the Sources of Poetry, new edit., Lawrence and Wishart, London, 1946, q.v.

[4] *Variété II*, pp. 261–2.

Number and Dream respectively I do not propose to draw any hard and fast line. In so far as Number partakes of the nature of logic and mathematics, and Dream partakes of the nature of nightmare, so far will they be mutually exclusive. But we have seen that even the closed systems seemed to possess a strange affinity by reason of the similarity of their structure, and the same thing will apply here, for Number and Dream are similar systems, being partly closed, in their tendency towards logic and nightmare, and partly open, in their tendency towards language. But an affinity may exist here more intimate than that which merely resides in similarity of structure. For in language these two partly open systems have a common ground. We might expect to find that, far from being mutually exclusive here, Number and Dream in proportion as they find their way into language draw closer and closer together. This appears to be exactly what does happen. The more fantastic and dream-like the meaning of what is being expressed in language, the more likely is Number to come in.

"And there appeared another wonder in heaven ; and behold a great red dragon, having seven heads and ten horns, and seven crowns upon his heads. And his tail drew the third part of the stars of heaven, and did cast them to the earth."

(Revelation xii, 3 and 4.)

"Seven of my sweet loves thy knife
Has bereaved of their life.
Their marble tombs I built with tears
And with cold and shuddering fears.

Seven more loves weep night and day
Round the tombs where my loves lay,
And seven more loves attend each night
Around my couch with torches bright."

(Blake, from *My phantom around me. . . .*)

"True Thomas lay on Huntlie Bank,
A ferlie spied he wi' his ee ;
There he saw a lady bright
Come riding down by the Eildon Tree.

Her skirt was o' the grass-green silk,
  Her mantle o' the velvet fine ;
At ilka tett o' her horse's mane
  Hung fifty siller bells and nine."

(*The Ballad of Thomas the Rhymer.*)

" On the fifth day of Christmas
My true love sent to me
Five gold rings
Four colly birds
Three French hens
Two turtle doves, and
A partridge in a pear tree."

(*The Twelve Days of Christmas.*)

" Five for the symbol at your door,
Four for the gospel-makers,
Three, three the rivals,
Two, two the lilywhite boys clothed all in green-o,
And one is one and all alone and ever more shall be so."

(*Green Grow the Rushes-O.*)

" The Song of One I know,
A rose its thorns between ;

The Song of Two I learned
Where only the birds have been ;

The Song of Three I heard
When March was fleet with hares ;

The Song of Four was the wind's—the wind's,
Where wheat grew thick with tares ;

The Song of Five, ah me !
Lovely the midmost one ;

The Song of Six, died out
Before the dream was done. . . .

One—two—three—four—five, six—
And all the grace notes given :
But *widdershins* and witchery-sweet,
Where is the Song of Seven ? "

(De La Mare, *The Song of Seven.*)
By kind permission.

" On the top of the Crumpetty Tree
The Quangle Wangle sat,
But his face you could not see
On account of his Beaver Hat.
For his Hat was a hundred and two feet wide,
With ribbons and bibbons on every side. . . ."

(Lear, *The Quangle Wangle's Hat.*)

No need to go any further. The connection between Number and Dream (quite apart from the fact that there may also be a connection between counting and sleep [1]—Sully speaks of " trying to fall asleep by means of the well-known device of counting ") [2] may from now on be considered justified.

Each, then, may be taken to be a valid mental system. For the moment it will be best to consider the common properties of the two, since, as with Language, any attempt to analyse either Number or Dream into simple units would be exceedingly difficult. Havelock Ellis and Freud both speak as if it were possible in the case of dreams,[3] but this seems very doubtful ; Freud himself later in the same work [4] emphasizes the complexity of the dream structure—" The dream thoughts . . . exhibit themselves as a psychical complex of the most complicated superstructure. Their parts stand in the most diverse relationship to each other ; they form backgrounds and foregrounds, stipulations, digressions, illustrations, demonstrations, and protestations ". The same thing, strangely enough, holds good in the case of Number. One might think that there was nothing easier than to analyse one of the ordinary numbers into simple units, but this apparent simplicity is deceptive. " The natural numbers seem to represent what is easiest and most familiar in

[1] Number and counting are not necessarily the same thing, but this need not affect the matter in hand here.

[2] James Sully, *Illusions* : A Psychological Study, Kegan Paul, Trench, and Co., 2nd edit., London, 1882, ch. vii, p. 130.

[3] Havelock Ellis, *The World of Dreams*, Constable and Co., Ltd., London, 1911, p. 16 : " Fantastic and marvellous as our dreams may sometimes be, they are in practically all cases made up of very simple elements."

Sigmund Freud, *On Dreams*, translated by M. D. Eder from the 2nd German edit., Heinemann, London, p. 11 : " It is an advantage to break up the dream into its elements and to search out the ideas which link themselves to each fragment."

[4] P. 56.

mathematics. But though familiar, they are not understood. Very few people are prepared with a definition of what is meant by 'number', or '0', or '1'. It is not very difficult to see that starting from 0, any other of the natural numbers can be reached by repeated additions of 1, but we shall have to define what we mean by 'adding 1', and what we mean by 'repeated'. These questions are by no means easy." [1]

In these circumstances of complexity, it will be more profitable to turn the attention to common properties rather than to attempt an analysis. This is analogous to the definition of a class by intension rather than by extension.[2] The whole process, the finding of common properties be it between classes themselves or members of classes, rests on the notion of similarity. This is particularly important because the principle of the recognition of similarity plays a decisive, though differing, part in each of the two systems Number and Dream, and may thereby serve as the means either of differentiation or of interrelation between them. For the present we shall be concerned with similarities between the two systems taken as a whole.

It has already been mentioned that each is a highly complex structure; this is one point of likeness. Another is that each system, while the mind is in it, is absolute, to be accepted on its own terms and without reference to anything else. Each is, in fact, a world of its own. The mind holds Number to be independent and infallible. "Figures do not lie, because they cannot lie. They cannot lie, because they have been declared *a priori* infallible. Having elected number as the sole arbiter for judging values, having agreed to abide by its decisions, we have *ipso facto* waived our right of appeal to any other tribunal." [3] "The

[1] Russell, *Introduction to Mathematical Philosophy*, George Allen and Unwin, Ltd., London, 1919, ch. i, p. 3.

[2] Ibid., ch. ii, p. 12: "A class or collection can be defined in two ways that at first sight seem quite distinct. We may enumerate its numbers. . . . Or we may mention a defining property. . . . The definition which enumerates is called a definition by 'extension', and the one which mentions a defining property is called a definition by intension. Of these two kinds of definition, the one by intension is logically more fundamental. This is shown by two considerations: (1) that the extensional definition can always be reduced to an intensional one; (2) that the intensional one often cannot even theoretically be reduced to the extensional one."

[3] Tobias Dantzig, *Number: The Language of Science*, George Allen and Unwin, Ltd., London, 1930, ch. xii, p. 244.

hypothesis that the whole numbers form a domain of individuals, hence a complete totality, is a fundamental requirement of ours." [1] The same thing is true of Dream. This, too, is a realm of its own. "We can never go behind the fantastic universe of our dreams. The validity of that universe is for dreaming consciousness unassailable. . . . We may puzzle over the facts presented to us; we may try to explain them; but it would be futile to deny them. . . . In dreams, it thus comes about, we accept the facts presented to us—that is the fundamental assumption of dream life." [2] Number and Dream each form a separate sphere for the mind, imposed and inviolable, a relation system that we can neither alter nor control. The properties of Number and the properties of Dream are things to be accepted, willy-nilly, by the mind. "When we say that we 'arrange' the numbers in these various orders, that is an inaccurate expression; what we really do is to turn our attention to certain relations between the natural numbers, which themselves generate such-and-such an arrangement. We can no more 'arrange' the natural numbers than we can the starry heavens; but just as we may notice among the fixed stars either their order of brightness or their distribution in the sky, so there are various relations among numbers which may be observed." [3] "We have no power over dreams." [4]

None the less, it must be borne in mind that each system is a system of mental concepts and nothing more. The fact that dreams are "the children of the brain" will not, probably, be called in question. Number, however, unless one is careful, may take on a delusive appearance of "reality". "The practical man demands an appearance of reality at least. Always dealing in the concrete, he regards mathematical terms not as symbols of thought but as images of reality." [5] This, too, is Russell's point when he

[1] D. Hilbert and P. Bernays, *Grundlagen der Mathematik*, Julius Springer, Berlin, 1934, § 1, p. 15.

[2] Havelock Ellis, op. cit., ch. iii, p. 64 and pp. 68–9.

[3] Russell, *Introduction to Mathematical Philosophy*, ch. iv, p. 30.

[4] Paul Radestock, *Schlaf und Traum*. Eine physiologisch-psychologische Untersuchung, Breitkopf und Härtel, Leipzig, 1879, ch. vi, p. 151.

[5] Dantzig, op. cit., ch. vii, p. 124.

says, " The number 2, in any other sense, is a metaphysical entity about which we can never feel sure that it exists or that we have tracked it down. It is therefore more prudent to content ourselves with the class of couples, which we are sure of, than to hunt for a problematical number 2, which must always remain elusive." [1] It is none the less strange, however, that we should be bound hand and foot in each of these two systems by mental cobwebs of our own spinning, and the result is that not merely do we lend the notion of " reality " to the cobwebs, but we may also imagine them to be imposed upon us from without. As far as Number is concerned, this would seem to be implicit in the phrase of the mathematician Kronecker, " Die ganze Zahl schuf der liebe Gott ; alles übrige ist Menschenwerk." [2] The same may be said about Dream. " Every dream is made up of action and reaction between a pseudo-universe and a freely-responding individual. On the one side there is the irresistibly imposed imagery—really, though we know it not, conditioned and instinctively moulded by our own organism—which stands for what in our waking hours we may term God and Nature ; on the other side is the soul struggling with all its might, and very inefficient means, against the awful powers that oppose it. The problem of the waking world is presented over again in this battle between the dreaming protagonist and his dreamed fate." [3] It is this, however, that links the universe of Number and that of Dream with the universe of day-to-day experience, where the same uncertainty as between the imposed and the self-imposed prevails. We ignore it in general, but it is there ; Russell says of the experience of seeing Sirius, " We do not eliminate the risk of error completely unless we confine ourselves to saying that an event of a certain sort is happening in the brain ; this statement may also be true, if we see Jupiter in a dream." [4]

[1] Russell, *Introduction to Mathematical Philosophy*, ch. ii, p. 18.

[2] Quoted by Hermann Weyl, *Philosophie der Mathematik und Naturwissenschaft*, Oldenbourg, Berlin, 1927, p. 27. (God made whole numbers ; all the rest is the work of man.)

[3] Havelock Ellis, op. cit., ch. iii, p. 60.

[4] Outline of Philosophy, p. 138, quoted by C. E. M. Joad, *Philosophical Aspects of Modern Science*, George Allen and Unwin, Ltd., London, 1932, ch. iii, p. 90.

This is the puzzle, already touched on in Chapter 7, that anything that exists is apparently thereby arbitrary. This is not to argue that numbers and dreams have a "real existence" that is not of this world; but in so far as the mind accepts them as systems in which to work, just so far have they an existence for that mind—and that existence is arbitrary. "There does not seem any logical necessity why there should be even one individual—why, in fact, there should be any world at all. . . . We seem driven to conclude that the existence of a world is an accident—i.e. it is not logically necessary."[1] As realms on their own, Number and Dream are no more and no less arbitrary than any other sphere of the mind, such as language, for instance. Valéry, speaking of prosody, says, "As for the arbitrary nature of these rules, it is in itself no greater than that of the rules of language, vocabulary, or syntax. . . . The exigencies of a strict prosody are the artifice which confers upon the natural language the properties of resistance, of matter that is alien to our spirit and, as it were, deaf to our desires. . . . We have to pursue words that do not always exist, and imagined coincidences; we have to maintain ourselves in a state of impotence, attempting to combine sound and significance, and creating in broad daylight one of those nightmares that exhaust the dreamer. . . . I have only wished to suggest that obligatory numbers, rhymes, fixed forms, all this element of the arbitrary, once they have been adopted, and set over against ourselves, possess a kind of personal and philosophic beauty."[2] This passage is interesting because it sets Number, Language, and Dream side by side, and seems to suggest that by the deliberate acceptance of the arbitrary limitations of each they may become the means of free construction. This may sound paradoxical, but the paradox is well attested in other spheres than these. The next stage will be to examine the "arbitrary limitations", or in other words, the defining characteristics of Number and Dream and then to see how these link up with language and poetry.

[1] Russell, *Introduction to Mathematical Philosophy*, ch. xviii, pp. 203 and 204.
[2] *Variété II*, pp. 61, 64–5, 66–7.

10. Number, Language and Dream

THE problem now is to map the relations holding between these three relation systems. Fig. 1 suggests the basic relationship between them. A complete map of Number would fall within the field of mathematics, that of Dream within the field of psychology, and each would fall outside the present terms of reference. Their interest here lies in their mixed nature, as systems partly closed and partly open. It seems necessary at this stage to define them for the purposes of this study. Plainly this will not be a complete definition of either, but the following will have to do :—

Number.—An infinite collection of complex mental concepts, forming an independent system of relations based largely on the principles of similarity and succession, which the mind employs to bring the relations of experience into order.

Dream.—An infinite collection of complex mental concepts, forming an independent system of relations based largely on the principles of similarity and succession, which the mind employs to bring the relations of experience into disorder.

In Chapter 9 Number and Dream were said to be opposites, it being in their connection with experience that the gulf between them lies ; but if the definitions given above are justified, this statement needs modification. They are opposites only in the sense that looking-glass reflections are opposites, with experience as the tangible object that casts the original image into these two mirrors. " What is important is the existence of *divergent* local and qualitative similarities, so that *two overlapping structures of networks of similarities cross each other* and arrange the same data in two different ways." [1] This is what happens here. Number and

[1] Jean Nicod, *Foundations of Geometry and Induction*, Kegan Paul, Trench, Trubner, and Co., Ltd., London, 1930, ch. iv, p. 84.

Dream form two networks of similarities and successions; these overlap in the field of experience, and since language and experience are co-extensive because of the fact of reference in language, the two networks should overlap in language as well, all of which would fit in with their nature as partly closed and partly open systems.

The two systems of Number and Dream have here been defined in terms of similarity and succession, and a little more must be said about the place held by each of these two principles in the systems concerned. They generate the relations by which Number and Dream hold together.

In the world of Number, the principle of succession is self-evident, and needs no expert justification. Indeed, one might have supposed that it was in itself sufficient as an explanation of the series of Natural Numbers. It is interesting to discover that this apparently is not so, and that similarity is a more fundamental principle in the nature of Number; "the notion of similarity is logically presupposed in the operation of counting, and is logically simpler though less familiar. . . ." [1] "The most elementary properties of numbers are concerned with one-one relations, and similarity between classes." [2] Both similarity and succession in Number are orderly and expected, that is, they tend to pull the system of Number, by the force of Order in the mind, into logic, where disorder and unexpectedness are unknown.

In the world of Dream, the principles of similarity and succession still hold good. Of the first of the two principles, it was known as long ago as Aristotle that "The most skilful interpreter of dreams is he who has the faculty of observing resemblances".[3] Havelock Ellis speaks of "this marked tendency in dreams to discover analogies" [4]; Freud says, "Only one of the logical relationships—that of *similarity*, *identity*, *agreement*—is found highly developed in the mechanism of dream formation." [5] As far as succession in

[1] Russell, *Introduction to Mathematical Philosophy*, ch. ii, p. 18.
[2] Ibid., ch. xviii, pp. 195–6.
[3] Aristotle, *De Divinatione per Somnum*, Eng. trans. edited by W. D. Ross, Clarendon Press, Oxford, 1931, vol. iii, ch. ii, p. 464*a*.
[4] Op. cit., ch. ii, p. 41, footnote.
[5] *On Dreams*, pp. 60–1.

dreams is concerned, Freud says, " *Causation* is represented by a *succession*, now by the sequence of the dreams, now by the immediate transformation of one image into another. In the great majority of cases, of course, causal relation is not expressed at all, but is obliterated by the sequence of elements which is unavoidable in the dream process." [1] Spitta also talks of " the relationship . . . of the simple, unconnected succession of the images ".[2] The point is that a sequence which is disorderly and unexpected is none the less a sequence. It works just like the Mad Hatter's riddle— " Why is a raven like a writing desk ? " There is no answer to the riddle, or at least none is given, but it turns upon the possibility of discovering an unexpected likeness in an unexpected sequence of two things.

It is now possible to go a step further. Similarity and succession have served so far as the means by which to map Number and Dream ; perhaps they may also map experience as well, since these two systems are partially connected with experience. The words of a mathematician may be helpful here ; he is talking about sounds in this particular case, but the words hold good for any form of data given by experience : " Succession arranges all the sounds in a single series ; on the other hand, similarity forms classes of sounds similar among themselves and different from all the others. Now these classes of similar sounds have their members dispersed in the order of time ; *the double structure which is introduced by this fact is perhaps the most fundamental feature of objective nature.* This mingling of successions and resemblances forms all physics. . . . The sensible universe . . . consists of *the same relations* : succession and global resemblance." [3] It looks as though these two principles may be quite as important in experience as they are in the systems of Number and Dream.

They have already acted successfully as a bridge between Number, Dream, and experience ; what about Language ? Since language and experience are tied together, the two principles ought to work in the system of Language as well ;

[1] *The Interpretation of Dreams*, p. 294.
[2] Op. cit., ch. vi, p. 183.
[3] Nicod, op. cit., pt. iii, ch. i, pp. 101 and 112.

and they do. In Chapter 4 the notion was put forward that words in their sound-look properties are stable, i.e. do not change, i.e. remain the *same*. Here is similarity. As for succession, it is obvious that this, in the case of Language, is syntax, and that upon it depends the whole possibility of talking sense. The subject is pleasantly treated in " Le Bourgeois Gentilhomme ", where the various permutations and combinations of the words, " Belle Marquise, vos beaux yeux me font mourir d'amour," are discussed at length. From the ordinary use of language we may move on to poetry ; here the questions of similarity and succession become even more capital. In these two lie buried the essential problems of poetry, the use of analogy, the question of poetic licence in word order, even the problems which might be labelled technical, rhyme, for instance. No wonder Valéry says, " What more subtle than the justification of the advantages of rhyme ? " [1]

In Chapter 5, poetry was said to be a number of words in a particular relationship. It is only according to the two principles of similarity and succession that the poet can draw words into that particular relationship ; succession and similarity in sound-look and reference are the only two things that the poet can control in language, and these only partially. Put it another way, and say that he must manipulate order and likeness in the sounds, and order and likeness in the images ; but likeness in the *words*, an annoying internal jingle in a line, for instance, induced by the sense, or order in the *words* as prescribed by usage and syntax, may be an intolerable nuisance.

Syntax in ordinary speech is very important, because it is the completion of the process described in Chapter 4, the endeavour to bring unity out of the variety of experience and so to make sense of it. In ordinary speech there are only two orders of similarity and succession to be taken into account, that of ordinary experience and that of syntax. All that is required is that the one shall conform to the other, that the two networks shall correspond. The result is useful and reliable—and wholly limited, in fact useful and reliable *because* wholly limited. This is Valéry's point

[1] *Variété IV*, NRF, Gallimard, Paris, 1938, p. 251.

when he says, " Their perceptions depend on a dictionary rather than on their retina. . . . They nourish themselves on concepts that are alive with words. (A general rule of this weakness existing in every department of knowledge is precisely the choice of *obvious* resting-places, of settling down in definite systems which make things easy, bring them within reach.) " [1] Repose in a definite system means, of course, repose in a limited system. So succession and similarity in language are tied to succession and similarity in experience, the stable word and the stable word-order result, and there, one might suppose, would be an end of the matter.

But the end is not yet ; for this is the point already touched on early in Chapter 4 : that this tidy, corresponding system of two networks is the poet's raw material. He can do nothing with it as it is, however. It must be freed in some way from its limiting factor if it is ever to become a means of free construction, and its limiting factor is its connection with experience. How is this to be shifted or broken ? As was seen in Chapter 4, it cannot be broken in the individual word, where sound-look and reference are indissolubly wedded. The only thing left to attack therefore is word-order. It was a poet himself, Ben Jonson, who said, " I am not of that opinion to conclude a Poet's liberty within the narrowe limits of lawes, which either the Grammarians, or Philosophers prescribe."

Assume for the moment that the poet will hold to similarity and succession as principles on which to work, but will at the same time abandon these principles as they appear in the mind's organization of ordinary language and hence as they appear in the mind's organization of ordinary experience. One may imagine as the starting-point a world of completely free word-order—a chaos naturally, a primitive disorder. This disorder is the first essential, for how can one make order unless there is disorder to make it from ? This is part of the poet's task : " In order that he, too, may bring into play his characteristic transformation, he must be provided with disorder ! " [2]

[1] *Variété*, p. 229.
[2] Valéry, *L'Idée Fixe*, NRF, Gallimard, Paris, 1934, p. 77.

Here is the necessary disorder. The problem now is how is it to be ordered. The answer is by the application of the principles of similarity and succession, but not as they appear in everyday experience, since this would merely organize the words back into ordinary speech again. The poet must look round for some other network of similarities and successions on which to build, and he turns to the two neighbouring systems of relations, the two that border on Language, namely Number and Dream, each of which has its own laws of similarity and succession. The fact that these laws are quite as arbitrary as those of language and experience does not matter in the least ; in fact, it may be an advantage, for they will provide new limiting factors and this is exactly what is required, for they will confer on language in poetry, as Valéry says, " les qualités d'une matière résistante." Total freedom would make any form of construction impossible ; the only choice open is the choice of limitations.

There are now two questions to be considered : How is the process of construction to be carried out and what is the aim of the process ?

The second question had better be considered first. Two aims have already been mentioned : that of abstracting language from the limitations of experience and that of making language from an open system into a closed one. (" Le monde du poème est essentiellement fermé et complet en lui-même.") Only two closed systems have been postulated here, Logic and Nightmare, the only two systems that bear no relation to experience. The characteristics of a closed system may be deduced from these two : perfect independence and self-sufficiency, equilibrium not subject to arbitrary forces, independence of the relations of normal experience. The extraordinary nature of the poet's task now comes to light, for language by nature is the exact opposite of these things. From it, by some miracle or magic, a system of relations is to be constructed which shall by the nature of its structure escape from the limitations of its medium. Poetry achieves this by calling in Number and Dream. The mind employs each system as a network by which to interpret the relations in experience. Number is used as a series of units by which to measure the continuum of time, for instance, to make time into something linear where things go along " one at a time " ; dream, on the other hand, has its own way of interpreting time, where it is perfectly possible for a thing to be two things at once, or where the dreamer can be in two places at once, and where what we normally think of as something stable, a collection of features making a face, for instance, is subject to " perpetual wane and change ", where nothing is ever the same for two moments running, where, in fact, similarity and succession, be it in the form of time or in another form, are different from those principles as known in experience. This is, of course, no less true of the numbering of time—but that is a problem for mathematicians. Linear time and simultaneity, number and dream, do not correspond with experience, and this is their advantage for the purposes of poetry ; for they offer alternative systems of organization, based on similarity and succession as language is, but not subject to the latter's limitations.

So the poet has three systems of relations to handle, Number, Language (in so far as he is not content to abandon normal syntax altogether), and Dream. From these three and the different uses to which they put succession and similarity, the cunning mind must weave another system, different again and perfect this time as none of these three are perfect, a sudden brief equilibrium stabilizing the forces of order and disorder in the mind, one moment of silence, timeless, perfect. By words to create silence—" Out of the inevitable conflict of images—inevitable, because of the creative, recreative, destructive, and contradictory nature of the motivating centre, the womb of war—I try to make that momentary peace which is a poem " [1] ; " literature attempts by ' words ' to create the condition of an absence of words." [2]—this would tally with all the remarks quoted in Chapter 5 on this point, silence being taken as the ultimate perfection. To make experience disappear (here surely is the connection between poetry and magic, " le vers, trait incantatoire ", " la merveille de

[1] Dylan Thomas, quoted by C. Day Lewis, *The Poetic Image*, Jonathan Cape, London, 1947, ch. v, p. 122.
[2] Valéry, *Mélange*, Gallimard, Canada, 1941, p. 131.

transposer un fait de nature en sa presque disparition vibratoire selon le jeu de la parole " [1]), to create nothing from something, to allow language, by the operation upon it of Number and Dream, to cancel itself out—this, no less, is the task of poetry. This is the aim ; and now the means also can be formulated more precisely. Language is itself a complex of two orders, sound-look and reference ; in the ordering of these two the technique of poetry must lie. *The poet employs the relations of Number to organize sound-look, the relations of Dream to organize reference.* This can only be a hypothesis at this stage, awaiting verification, but it seems to be a promising one.

It was suggested in Chapter 5 that Mallarmé and Rimbaud tried to pull Language towards infinity (i.e. out of time and space) in opposite directions ; if the hypothesis given above is right, and if each poet went to an opposite extreme, then we should expect to find Mallarmé abandoning dream and reference for logic as the road to silence, via number and sound-look, and Rimbaud abandoning number and logic for nightmare as the road to silence via dream and reference. The fact that Valéry writes continually of Mallarmé in such terms as " an essentially formal genius, rising little by little to the abstract conception of the whole range of combinations of figures and devices " [2] the whole of *Un Coup de Dés*, the remark of a critic of Rimbaud that " terror came upon him, the terror which comes when we leave the world of Number and peer into the gulf over which that fragile scaffolding has been flung ",[3] Rimbaud's evolution into free verse, the absence in Mallarmé's poems of words with a strongly visual element in their reference and their abundance in Rimbaud's work—all these begin to take on new and interesting possibilities. They will be dealt with in Part II.

[1] From *Divagations*. " The line of poetry, a stroke of incantation " ; " the marvel of transposing a fact of nature into its near-disappearance in vibration according to the play of words."

[2] *Variété II*, p. 182.

[3] Edgell Rickword, *Rimbaud : The Boy and the Poet*, Heinemann, Ltd., London, 1924, ch. xvi, p. 177.

Summary of Part I

LANGUAGE is a double relationship system, a sound-look system in constant but arbitrary connection with a system of reference. The former is stable, the latter variable within certain limits. The fact that language has meaning entails an unavoidable connection with experience. It follows that language by its very nature and purpose can never form a perfect system, since perfection and completeness can be reached only at the level of pure abstraction in the mind, which language can never reach. Ultimate perfection must lie outside the mind altogether ; the nearest approximation to it can be reached by following in their respective directions the two forces in the mind, the one tending towards order, the other towards disorder. The extreme of the force of order is Logic, which is order and excludes disorder ; the extreme of the force of disorder is Nightmare, which is disorder and excludes order. These are the only two closed systems of the mind, closed because they are in stable equilibrium resulting from the balance of the two forces by the total exclusion of one, and therefore not subject to arbitrary external interference ; necessity and not chance governs these two systems. Overlapping with Logic and Nightmare are Number and Dream respectively, systems which are partly closed in so far as they partake of the nature of the two former systems, but also partly open in that they overlap into the field of language, which is also that of experience. Language is an open system, subject to arbitrary order and disorder. The aim of poetry is to create from Language a closed relation system by resolution of the two forces of order and disorder, not by the total exclusion of one or other but by utilizing each so that each may cancel the other out and a momentary equilibrium be formed. This is done by adopting the two neighbouring relationship systems of Number and Dream and re-interpreting the principles of similarity and succession in Language according to the use made of these two principles in these other two systems, which are looking-glass reflections of each other both in their relation structure of similarity and succession and the application of this structure to experience. The poet abandons the relations of similarity and succession as proffered to him by experience and ordinary language ; and by the organization of one half of Language, sound-look, according to Number's system of similarity and succession, and the organization of the other half, reference, according to Dream's system of similarity and succession, he seeks to create a perfect system on its own, out of time and space—that emptiness and silence which shall be the final beauty.

PART II

11. Introduction to Part II

" If you stop to consider the work you have done
  And to ask what your labour is worth, dear,
Angels may come for you, Willie my son,
  But you'll never be wanted on earth, dear."

(Kipling, *Mary's Son.*)

PART I of this piece of work began with the suspicion—one could call it no more than that, since at that stage the work had not yet begun to grow—that the technique of analysis was unlikely to be helpful in any inquiry into the nature of language and poetry. Now Part I is finished, and with Part II the inquiry moves into a different stage. Here, also, the work has still to grow and it is difficult to be wise before the event. This is clearly, however, a halfway house, and questions of the method of inquiry are perhaps even more pertinent than they were at the beginning. This is not going to be a post-mortem into Part I, Kipling's warning given above being a very sound one. It is directed forward, towards the as yet potential Part II.

What is presumably the approved method of research, the dissection of the material into individual detail which may then be classified and from which deductions may be drawn, has three things to be said for it : it is safe, disciplined, and reputable. The method employed here is plainly not this one. One may fairly conclude, therefore, that it is likely to be unsafe and undisciplined ; I fear there is no question at all about its being disreputable. With the shift from Part I to Part II, and the introduction of a new aspect of the subject-matter, the poetry of Mallarmé and Rimbaud, an opportunity might present itself of redeeming the unsafeness, indiscipline, and disreputability of the method employed in Part I. The question is one of real importance, because the choice of method or form will throw light not only on the validity or invalidity of the results so far achieved but also on the nature of the subject-matter itself. In short, form and content are here inextricably mixed up, or, to put it another way, are merely two aspects of the same process. If wrong, the method of inquiry ought to lead either to sterility, as a wrongly directed train of thought does, or to palpable falsehood. If right, the method should prove fruitful in the mind—but it will go further than that.

Anyone who writes poetry knows that an image or set of sensations or whatever it may be that says to the mind " I could be made into a poem " demands of its own accord its own rhythm and rhyme-scheme, its own particular form of organization. The demand is apparently arbitrary, but is not to be denied ; it would be utter waste of time, for instance, to attempt to transform into blank verse a poetical subject that suggested for itself alternately rhyming 4 and 3 stress lines. The writer need not see consciously the inner significance of the form at the time, being merely aware that the work has demanded it and the demand must be met as well as may be. But if the poem, after the necessary hard intellectual work on the part of its writer, starts to grow and rounds itself off into a satisfactory whole, it is meaningless to say that it ought to have been written in another metre.

In this respect a piece of poetry and a piece of research need not necessarily differ. The data in each case are a subject or some particular grouping of material, and a mind. The approved method of critical inquiry mentioned earlier apparently regards the process of organization as one-way, viz. the attempt by a mind to organize a raw mass of material. But this is only half the process, which is two-way and not one-way. The mind must certainly wrestle with its subject-matter, pull it to pieces, select and reject ; but once this is done, or while it is still in the doing, *what* is to be said will take command imperiously and determine for the mind *how* it is to be said. If the double process has been successfully established, and mind and material have each been subjected to the discipline of the other, the resulting work should be such that the form, method, or technique employed, the organization system inherent in the work, is not merely a vehicle for the presentation of the subject-matter ; it has its own significance, because the subject-matter required from the mind in question that one form and that only, in which to grow into the final work which is the reciprocal product of material on a mind and a mind on material.

To study the form that certain material demands of a mind for its own growth (and for the mind's growth as well, strangely enough) is to study the innermost nature of that material—and probably of the mind also, though that is not the point here. The mind itself may prove inadequate to the demands made on it, may grow tired,

> " Wander loose and sigh
> Through the turbid blue,"

and direct its attention elsewhere. But one thing it cannot do : it cannot undertake the work, i.e. submit itself to the discipline of the particular material, and at the same time ignore or flout the nature of that discipline. This discipline concerns the particular material and the particular mind, and them alone. But once the mind has accepted the form of organization imposed on it by the material, then it is in a position to begin to understand the nature of the material ; for the organization is a potential relation system, and once the mind has perceived it, the system which that mind will construct may interpret the nature of the subject-matter. This is much the same thing that Poincaré is talking about when he says, " Mathematicians proceed therefore ' by construction ', they ' construct ' combinations that are more and more complicated. Then, returning by the analysis of these combinations and wholes, so to speak, to their primitive elements, they perceive the relations of these elements and deduce from them the relations of the wholes in their turn." [1] But there can be no set form of inquiry. The particular mind must grope about among the particular intractabilities of its material. Perhaps it is a hard fate to be called on to play croquet with a hedgehog for a ball and a flamingo for a mallet, but experiment is the only possible method of procedure.

[1] *La Science et l'Hypothèse*, pt. i, ch. i, p. 26.

The analogy of the process with a game is a helpful one, because it brings the problem of relation systems, and the rules on which they work, down to a more approachable level, and it puts the problem where it should be, outside controversy. "There can be no scepticism with regard to the rules of a game." [1] In Part I of this book the game has been to construct slowly and by stages a way of thinking about poetry. The principal rule was that the thinking must be consistent as far as the player could tell. So the inquiry, as poetry does, resolved itself into the attempt to construct an independent and consistent system out of certain data, here the particular subject matter and the particular mind.

It would be unfitting to make either claims or apologies for the system as it now stands; one is reminded once more of Kipling's Willie. The dangers of playing one's own game are apparent, but there seems no reason to suppose that in the second half the rules will be changed, or that the particular hedgehogs and flamingoes involved (meaning no discourtesy to the two poets who are to be the main material of Part II) will not once more, as in Part I, impose their own game upon the player. That the rules are not the accepted rules of croquet is a pity; but no other way of proceeding is possible, for two reasons. First, the rules of this game conform to the particular data, here the subject-matter and the mind involved. This, it may be said, may only be proof of the weaknesses of both, the intractability of a subject that will not submit to analysis, classification, and deduction (one is tempted to add Ambition, Distraction, Uglification, and Derision also), and the indiscipline of a mind that shies away from necessary drudgery. This may very well be true, but even so it is at best only an indictment of the data. The second reason is this: even though it may be presumption to attempt to construct one's own way of thinking, yet this way of going to work will do what no other can do, will offer by its own nature a possible interpretation of the material in hand—poetry, which is also an attempt by a mind, not to analyse the complex into simples and then set about construction, but to manipulate the complex and construct from it an independent system.

[1] Valéry, *Variété IV*, p. 46.

Surely research also may legitimately be regarded as an artistic enterprise.

I do not mean that the method will offer an interpretation of the *poems*. Mallarmé and Rimbaud have suffered quite enough already by being interpreted. My own view is that to demand an interpretation of a poem is evidence of misunderstanding of the nature of poetry. All one can ask is admission to the world of the poem, and permission to explore. With luck, and with a good poem, the world to be explored will never be capable of complete interpretation, because it has to resolve both forces in the mind, the force towards order and the force towards disorder. And if both are regarded as equally valuable, any interpretation of a poem, which would result in total comprehension, i.e. total inclusion in the realm of order, would be a distortion and worse still an impoverishment.

The next stage will be an inquiry into the problem of how it would be possible to make language into nothingness, as Mallarmé tried to do, or into everythingness, as Rimbaud tried to do. The emphasis will be on these two as extreme cases rather than on any hypothetical common ground between them ; but it is possible that at the same time some light may be thrown on other possibilities that there may be for poetry besides, or rather between, these two extremes. It is on this basis that Part II will accordingly proceed.

12. Prose and Poetry

IT is now possible to collect some of the things that were said here and there in Part I, and to work them together. In Chapter 3 a tentative plan of action was put forward, in which words were to be considered under three heads, first as individuals, then as small groups, and lastly in "larger groups making a whole, e.g. a poem". The consideration of words as individuals occupied Chapters 4 and 5; words in groupings and the relationships involved provided the starting point for Chapters 6 to 10; the time has now come when we can move on to the third stage and consider the poem as such.

In Chapter 5, poetry, and hence, of course, also the poem, was said to be "a number of words". This is true enough, but as we know, a number of words need not be poetry—it may be prose. For language is primarily a convenience in the process of communication, applied directly to experience, and for the mind practically indistinguishable from it, while poetry is not; "lyric poetry is absolutely no use, and poetry generally is almost no use." [1] Faced with these two apparently rival organizations of language into prose and poetry, we need to be sure that we have disentangled the essential differences between them before going any further.

Chapter 4 set out some of the ways in which language, or prose, may be used as a tool for ordering experience. Briefly, the process is that since words have reference to experience, the mind can use them to isolate (apparently), and classify experience, rendered abstract by its transformation into language and hence capable of mental organization. In Chapter 5 the phrase was used: "the ordinary mind

[1] E. M. Forster, *Anonymity: An Enquiry*, Hogarth Essays, Hogarth Press, London, 1925, p. 10.

brings order out of the chaos of experience with the help of language."

That was near enough to the mark at that stage, but it needs to be looked into more closely now, because as it stands it suggests that the mind is active in the process. This is just what it is not. Ordinary language or prose—word plus reference, conventional syntax, sense—is a ready-made system into which the mind is born, so to speak, and in which it is brought up. Vocabulary, syntax, the making of sense (i.e. the corresponding with common experience), which form the elements, relation-system and final aim of the system of language called prose, are not constructed by the individual mind, they are adopted. " It is . . . thought which has to run into the mould of the sentence and adapt itself to the order of the words." [1] The mind need not construct anything ; it takes over a labour-saving system to save itself the trouble of having to construct. Once the system is memorized and the rules of the game learnt, no further effort is needed. The process appears to be something like this : a succession of letters and sounds is recognized by the mind as a familiar remembered unit ; in connection with the units the mind automatically remembers a reference. In the sentence each unit represents a class (noun, verb, etc.). The mind recognizes the class-succession as familiar, and the remembered references in this order are accepted by the mind as being in accordance with remembered experience, i.e. as making sense. The whole process attains the maximum of success when the minimum of effort is required. This explains the fact, noted by Valéry, that the mind forgets the language immediately if it has understood the reference ; " our memory repeats to us the speech that we have not understood. Repetition corresponds with incomprehension. *It shows us that the function of language has been frustrated.*" [2]

All this is accepted by the mind as a convention, enabling experience (which, as was seen in Chapter 4, is assumed to

[1] Albert Dauzat, *La Philosophie du Langage*, Flammarion, Paris, 1917, bk. i, ch. i, p. 13.

[2] *Variété III*, p. 81. Cf. also the remarks in Chapter 5 on an absence of reference coupled with sonority in a word which makes it stick in the memory.

be uniform between individuals) to be classified, labelled, and communicated. If the three-fold nature of the process, words via syntax to sense, is accepted in full, then prose provides, as it were, a prefabricated universe for the mind, superimposed by the fact of reference upon the universe of experience—whatever that may be, for as Valéry's *Monsieur Teste* says, " l'univers n'existe que sur le papier," [1] and for the mind it is built up out of language. This is Wittgenstein again : " The limits of my language are the limits of my world."

The data in prose, or the rules of the game, are not merely, as one might suppose at first, words and a mind, which look like the same data as those of poetry. The data are three, combined in one system : words—syntax—sense. The words are given since the mind does not invent them. The sense is given in that it has to conform to common experience. The syntax is given as the conventional linear order in space and time in which the words must be marshalled if sense is to be achieved, and if the connection between language and experience, for which language exists, is to be maintained.

The data of prose may now be seen in all their complication. Prose is a conventional system, triple-jointed, with a double connection with experience ; at the first stage because words have reference, and at the third stage because prose make sense. This double connection is very important, because it means that the universe of prose is doubly tied to the universe of experience, and this, of course, admits into language all the complexity of the universe of experience. Carnap talks about " the incredibly complicated word-language ". [2] No wonder language is so hard to think about clearly.

Alongside the statement that the universe of prose is coextensive with the universe of experience one may set three quotations, about poetry this time, the first two from Mallarmé, the third from Valéry about Mallarmé.

[1] Nouvelle édition augmentée de fragments inédits, NRF, Paris, 1946, p. 107. (The universe exists only on paper.)

[2] Rudolf Carnap, *The Logical Syntax of Language*, Kegan Paul, Trench, Trubner, and Co., Ltd., London, 1937, Introd., p. 8.

"J'ai pris ce sujet d'un sonnet nul et se réfléchissant de toutes les façons, parce que mon œuvre est si bien préparé et hiérarchisé, représentant comme il le peut, l'Univers, que je n'aurais su, sans endommager quelqu'une de mes impressions étagées, rien en enlever." [1]

"Fragile, comme est mon apparition terrestre, je ne puis subir que les développements absolument nécessaires pour que l'univers retrouve, en moi, son identité. Ainsi, je viens, à l'heure de la Synthèse, de délimiter l'œuvre qui sera l'image de ce développement." [2]

"C'est ainsi qu'il est venu à vouloir donner à l'art d'écrire un sens universel, *une valeur d'univers*." [3]

There is an echo here of Rimbaud's words which were quoted in Chapter 5: "The time of a universal language will come!"

Poetry, then, or more properly a poem, may be regarded as a universe, too. This is not just fanciful or metaphoric language. A poem is a world of its own, quite as much so as the other worlds of the mind we have already looked at, logic, for instance, or dream. They all turn upon the same axis. "Do you admit the existence of a mental effort tending to produce or construct . . . or rather, to let a whole order, a whole system, produce itself, one part of which, or perhaps certain conditions, are given?" [4] This is exactly what happens with a poem. Certain conditions are given, but, as we shall see in a moment, these are not precisely similar to the data of prose. There is another and more fundamental difference between prose and poetry, however. In prose

[1] Stephane Mallarmé, *Propos sur la Poésie*, recueillis et présentés par Henri Mondor. Editions du Rocher, Monaco, 1946. Letter to Henri Cazalis, 18th July, 1868, p. 84.

I have taken this subject from a sonnet that is null, reflecting itself every way, because my work is so certain in its preparation and hierarchy, representing, as best it may, the Universe, that I should not have known how to take anything out without damaging one or another of my impressions ranged one above another.

[2] Ibid., letter to Henri Cazalis, 18th July, 1868, p. 84.

Fragile as my terrestrial apparition is, I can only undergo the developments that are absolutely necessary for the Universe to find once again its identity in me. Thus at the moment of Synthesis, I have just mapped out the work that will be the image of this development.

[3] *Variété II*, p. 218.

It was in this way that he came to wish to give the art of writing a universal significance, *a value of a universe*.

[4] Valéry, *L'Idée Fixe*, p. 171. (The dots in the sentence are his.)

the mind is passive, accepting the conventional vehicle of language without question. In poetry the mind is active, having to make its own system. This point needs to be emphasized, in view of statements such as this one: " When, as in poetry, words are used not as symbols but as specific drugs to create images and produce emotional response in the reader or hearer, the words can no longer be given their proper meaning and the ordinary symbolic process is frustrated."[1] The point of view that poetry is a " dull opiate to the brain " is surely mistaken. Poetry is the exact opposite; in fact, the " specific drug " is not poetry, it is prose.

In both systems the basic elements are the same: words and a mind. The words are the same, sound-look plus reference, each little group of letters and sounds bringing in at the door with it its inevitable accompaniment of reference to experience. In poetry and prose, as happened in Vachel Lindsay's *Daniel Jazz*, it is impossible to separate the callers and their properties :—

> " Old man Ahab leaves his card.
> Elisha and the bears are a-waiting in the yard.
> Here comes Pharaoh and his snakes a-calling.
> Here comes Cain and his wife a-calling.
> Shadrach, Meschach and Abednego for tea.
> Here comes Jonah and the whale,
> And the *Sea* ! "

Given even a few words, it is a case of Here comes the universe a-calling.

This is quite enough to have on one's hands, doubtless; but in the case of poetry this is the sum-total of the given conditions, and this is again where poetry differs from prose. For from these words the poet may, indeed must, construct his own system. It must be " tout un ordre, tout un système ", a universe on its own. Neither common syntax nor the making of sense need be given conditions. Each poem must be an independent self-sufficient and closed system, constructed in its own particular way, with its own premises, development, and conclusion, its own

[1] W. H. Watson, *On Understanding Physics*, p. 34.

logic, in fact. " One could conceive of poetic language developing to a pitch where it would constitute a system of notations as different from practical language as are those of the artificial languages of algebra or chemistry. The least poem contains all the germens and indications of this possible development." [1]

This poem-universe will, like the universe of prose, have a potential double connection with the universe of experience, but the nature of the connection will be different. A poem starts, as prose does, with the connection between words and experience implicit in the fact of reference ; but since this is what makes language an open system, and the aim of the poet is to create a closed system, this connection must be attenuated in some way. This cannot be done at the level of the words themselves because the connection between sound-look and reference in the individual word or phrase cannot be shifted. It could only be done by distracting the mind's attention from that connection. How this might be achieved will be discussed later.

In a poem, too, as in prose, there will be a connection between the system when finally constructed and complete, the finished poem-universe, and the universe of experience. But it is not the connection between prose and experience. That was achieved by superimposition, fitting one system on to the other so that they tallied as exactly as possible, achieving a total interdependence. The poem-universe, on the contrary, aims at total independence. But in so far as it is a separate detached independent system, it might be set side by side with the universe of experience and offer possibilities of interpretation of the latter, not by identity of form but by analogy between forms. In either case the interpretation will turn upon form.[2] The universe of number is used in just this way to interpret experience ; we could

[1] Paul Valéry, *Pièces sur l'Art*, NRF, Gallimard, Paris, 1934, p. 49.

[2] This may be perhaps because form is our only method of comparison. Cf. Eddington, *The Philosophy of Physical Science*, p. 142. " Our knowledge of structure is communicable, whereas much of our knowledge is incommunicable. Therefore, there is no way of comparing my sensation of the taste of mutton with your sensation of the taste of mutton. . . . But if we are both looking at a landscape, although there is no way of comparing our visual sensations as such, we can compare the *structures* of our respective visual impressions of the landscape."

conceivably use the universe of dream for the same purpose if we had the mind, or the wit. "It may well be, we may add, that the dream process furnishes the key to the metaphysical and even, indeed, the physical problems of our waking thoughts." [1]

The analogy, however, between Number and Dream on the one hand and Poetry on the other as possible interpreters of experience is not a perfect one, because Number and Dream are systems partly open and partly closed. Experience is an open system, and one might expect that whereas it would have some affinities with Number and Dream because of their mixed character, it would have none with closed systems. This holds good with the two closed systems already postulated, Logic and Nightmare. It is of the essence of these systems that they exclude any connection with experience; this is what makes them what they are. Now a poem, too, if properly constructed, is a closed system, achieving this result, as we saw in Chapter 8, by a perfect if only momentary equilibrium. But it is constructed from precisely the same elements as those which the mind attaches to experience, i.e. words, and in this way offers something unique, the transformation of language (which is the mind's expression of experience) from something imperfect, the open systems of prose and experience, into something perfect, the closed system of a poem. There may be more than one had at first supposed in the poet's words—"And in short measures life may perfect be"—life, be it noted, not language. This links up with magic again.

Between the two connections with experience in the systems of prose and poetry comes a certain serial order in the words. This may be called syntax, but if so the term must be interpreted widely; "one would have to give to 'syntax' a very wide interpretation, that of the study of the whole system of relations that can be established between the different words in a sentence or line of verse, perhaps even of a bigger whole—a page or a poem." [2] It is necessary to postulate at once two syntaxes, that of

[1] Havelock Ellis, op. cit., ch. iii, p. 63.
[2] Jacques Scherer, op. cit., p. 79.

prose which we have known from our youth up, and that of poetry, about which anyone who writes poetry will have glimmerings, but which is not taught in the schools. Carnap defines syntax as " concerned, in general, with the *structure of possible serial orders* (of a definite kind) *of any elements whatsoever* ".[1] He goes on to say, " The syntactical investigation of a system which is already given is indeed a purely mathematical task." [2] This is upheld by Valéry who speaks of " la Syntaxe, qui est calcul," [3] and one is again in a difficulty for lack of mathematical training. One thing at least is plain—there has been a restricting of the ground to be covered ; we are no longer concerned with poetry but with the poem. The poetic mind may work by " shedding forth universes ", but our immediate concern will be neither that mind nor the process of creation, but the finished universes, the poems produced.

[1] Op. cit., Introd., § 2, p. 6.
[2] Ibid., pt. v, § 86, p. 332.
[3] *Variété III*, p. 12. (Syntax, which is calculation.

13. Everythingness, Nothingness, and Poetry

" L'Art se limite à l'infini, et y commençant ne peut progresser."
(From " *Le Ten o'clock de M. Whistler*,"
translated by Mallarmé.) [1]

IT is obvious that extremism is a form of simplification. Faced with a vast collection of poem-universes, all differing in character and intention and hence in methods of construction, we are not going to attempt to elucidate for the moment the nature of these intermediate universes which maintain varying degrees of balance between order and disorder, between construction of the poem universe and destruction of the prose universe. In this topsy-turvy world, a " simple " poem such as " My love is like a red red rose " would set far greater problems than the most hermetic poem of Mallarmé or Rimbaud, because these two poets adopted the final simplification of becoming extremists themselves, one at one extreme, one at the other. For this reason the simplicity of their respective complications provides a starting point from which to move towards understanding the complexities of apparently more simple poems.

This paradox was stated at the end of Chapter 5, and there, too, a suggestion was put forward as to the nature of the extremism of these two poets, Rimbaud trying to get everything into language, Mallarmé trying to get everything out. To rephrase this slightly in the light of subsequent inquiries : Rimbaud was trying to create a poem-universe that should contain everything, every thing ; Mallarmé to create a poem-universe which should contain nothing, no thing. With the two extremes of All and None to

[1] " Art finds its limits at infinity, and taking its origin there can make no progress."

consider, we can shelve for the present the consideration of Some, which is where the greatest complexity lies.

When originally putting forward the suggestion about the absolute nature of the aims of these two poets, I said that either must seem incredible to the rational mind. But as with so many other things in this inquiry, the only way to progress is to take these aims seriously, as Rimbaud and Mallarmé did. Various quotations were brought forward in Chapter 5 from the prose works of each to support the suggestion. More could now be added to these, particularly Mallarmé's continual references to "le Néant" in his letters [1]; but the evidence must lie ultimately not in the theory of either poet but in his practice. Before their poems are considered, however, one preliminary question will have to be answered: Suppose one set out with the same intention as Rimbaud or Mallarmé—to create a poem-universe that would contain everything, or nothing, how could it be done? The question is to be taken quite seriously, because not until it is answered shall we know what to look for in the poems of these two.

First of all we must see what our notions of everythingness and nothingness amount to, and then see how language might be manipulated so as to come as near to them as possible. Here, arrived at from a different angle, are the two initial data of poetry as stated in the last chapter, viz. a mind, and words. The mind constitutes a difficulty at once, because it cannot imagine either everythingness or nothingness. "If we must have some idea of a nothingness the idea of nothing is nothing; or rather it is already something. . . . We obscurely imagine that *everything* is

[1] Cf. *Propos sur la Poésie*, letter to Henri Cazalis, March, 1866, p. 59. "Malheureusement, en creusant le vers à ce point, j'ai rencontré deux abîmes, qui me désespèrent. L'un est le Néant, auquel je suis arrivé sans connaître le Bouddhisme et je suis encore trop désolé pour pouvoir croire même à ma poésie et me remettre au travail, que cette pensée écrasante m'a fait abandonner."

Letter to Henri Cazalis, 14th May, 1867, p. 79. "J'ai fait une assez longue descente au Néant" . . . etc.

Unhappily, in digging down into the poetry to this point, I have come upon two abysses which drive me to despair. The one is Nothingness, which I have happened upon without any knowledge of Buddhism, and I am still too overcome to be able to believe even in my poetry or to get back to the work which this shattering notion has made me abandon.

I have made a comparatively long descent into Nothingness. . . .

something, and so we imagine *something* and call it *everything*." [1] Unable to grapple with All or Nothing, the mind falls back on Some. Words, too, produce the same sort of difficulty. Since a poem is a number of words, i.e. a limited series of words, obviously no poem can contain no words, even if those unheard are sweeter, or alternatively all words and the references they bring with them,

. . . " Flit would the ages
  On soundless wings
Ere unto Z
  My pen drew nigh ;
Leviathan told,
  And the honey-fly :
And still would remain
  My wit to try—
My worn reeds broken,
  The dark tarn dry " . . .

So we must put the question a little differently and ask how a limited mind can most nearly imagine everythingness and nothingness and express its imagination in the limited medium of language.

First, how can one imagine an everythingness, so to speak? (though this sounds like the Dormouse's question, " Did you ever see such a thing as a drawing of a muchness ? "). It will have to be a universe containing as many things as possible, and since, as we have seen, the actual number of things will inevitably be limited, each thing must connect with as many other things as possible. It will be a universe in which everything is related to everything else in every possible way, and everything in this universe must be included as significant and relevant, i.e. related into the whole. Ideally it would make one perfect system in which each thing was related wholly and perfectly to every other thing. The main characteristics of this universe, then, are that it is all-embracing and multiply inter-related. The more possibilities of relations there are in its elements the better, i.e. the more complex they are by nature, the better. Now the elements here, since the universe is to be a poem,

[1] Valéry, *Variété*, pp. 130 and 132.

are words. Of the two systems, sound-look and reference, which make up language, sound-look is going to be too simple to be of much help in constructing a universe of everythingness. A simple linear succession of sounds and letters does not offer very great possibilities for this complex organization. But what about reference, which is wedded to the whole complex of experience, where one image cannot be separated from another in the mind, where each brings with it numbers of other images and references, so that there is no reason why there should ever be an end to the associative chain so called up? This offers immense possibilities, and the closer it is held to experience at this stage the better, because in general the words with the greatest potentiality of association and relatedness with others are those discussed in Chapter 4 under the heading " Stable word plus stabilized diversity of reference ", words with direct reference to sense experience. So in this poem-universe of everythingness we should expect to find many words of this kind, and, holding them all together, a network of relatedness, so that none of the images are unconnected and none of the connections between the images are without significance, where there is a reason for everything being there because it links up with everything else into one whole system.

But this is nothing original, nor is there anything here to surprise the mind, which is perfectly familiar with this process of weaving everything into complex patterns and seeing new significances in the multiple ways in which things are related one to another. For this is nothing other than the world of Nightmare (and of certain types of madness) where everything becomes significant, nothing is excluded, and where, from the totality of its impressions however apparently ill-fitting and incongruous, the mind weaves a vast new universe. 'I recognize it in myself by this characteristic: that all the possible objects of the ordinary world, exterior or interior, beings, events, feelings, and actions, remaining normal as far as appearances are concerned, suddenly fall into a relationship that is indefinable but wonderfully in harmony with the modes of our general perceptions. This is to say that these things, these familiar beings—or rather the ideas that represent them—change their value in some sort. They call up one another, they are associated quite differently from usual ; they become (if I may be allowed the expression) *musicalized*, acquiring resonances, the one against the other, corresponding in their harmonies, as it were. The poetic universe defined in this way presents considerable analogies with what we may surmise of the universe of dream." [1] From the normal things, sense-impressions and images of experience (which is what language largely consists of as far as reference is concerned), the dreamer builds up a new and all-embracing universe. " In dreams, everything is automatically included, nothing left out." [2] This is the ultimate conclusion of Baudelaire's Correspondances, where " Les parfums, les couleurs et les sons se répondent " (perfumes, colours, and sounds correspond with one another), of Rimbaud's dream of " un verbe poétique accessible, un jour ou l'autre, à tous les sens " (a poetic language accessible, one day or other, to all the senses). Everything will have a new meaning because it will be inter-related with everything else, and this eliminates chance because any apparently chance addition, as can be seen in dreams, for instance, is at once woven into the whole, no matter how fantastic the finished product may be. The process is described to perfection by someone who was at once a poet and a madman, Gérard de Nerval. It is most interesting to see how his words fit in with those of Valéry just quoted, also a poet, but very sane.[3] " I attributed a mystic sense to the conversations of the warders and of my companions. It seemed to me that they represented all the nations of the world, and that between us we had to regulate in a new way the paths of the stars and to widen the bounds of the solar system. . . . My rôle seemed to me to be the re-establishing of universal harmony. . . . This thought led to another : that there existed a vast cabal of all living creatures, with the aim of

[1] Valéry, *Poésie et Pensée Abstraite*, Zaharoff Lecture for 1939, Clarendon Press, Oxford, 1939, p. 8.

[2] Valéry, *Variété II*, p. 262.

[3] Cf. Havelock Ellis, op. cit., ch. x, p. 273. " We may say that the man of genius is in closer touch with the laws of the dream world than is the ordinary civilized man."

re-establishing the world in its primal harmony, and that communication took place by means of the magnetism of the stars; that an unbroken chain linked those minds the world over that were dedicated to this universal communication; and songs, dances, glances of the eye, magnetized from one to the next, interpreted the same aspiration. . . . The whole of nature took on a new appearance. The speech of my companions was turned in mysterious ways of which I understood the meaning. Even formless and lifeless objects lent themselves to my mental calculations. And from collections of pebbles, shapes of angles or cracks or openings, from patterns of leaves, from colours, scents, and sounds I sensed harmonies emerging, unknown till then." [1]

To sum up, then: if the poet is going to create a universe of everythingness, the only possible thing to do is to come as close as possible to creating a nightmare, "creating in broad daylight one of those nightmares that exhaust the dreamer." [2] This has to be done with words, but the emphasis will be on reference and the complexity of its organization rather than on sound-look. Sound-look and reference cannot, indeed, be separated, and the references from which the nightmare is to be built will have to be called up by their corresponding groups of letters and sounds. But the mind will have to be distracted from sound-look to reference by the insistent demands of the latter for attention, and this will turn largely upon the concreteness of the reference and its closeness to experience. These, then, are the pointers we shall make use of in our examination of Rimbaud's poetry.

We now come to the second question: how to construct a universe of nothingness, a universe containing no thing. As a poem-universe, this, too, will have to start with words, sound-look, and reference (which brings with it all the things in experience), and a mind. We cannot start from nothingness; the nothingness will have to be of the kind where the things that were there have disappeared. There

[1] *Aurélia*, Edition: Le Rêve et la Vie, Payot, Paris, 1913, pt. ii, ch. vi, p. 140 *et seq.*
[2] Valéry, *Variété*, p. 65.

will, as in the everything-universe, be a relationship system, but unlike that universe, the relations will connect not things but nothing. It will be like the old joke about the fish-net—a lot of holes held together with string. This is how Mallarmé puts it : " Nous savons, captifs d'une formule absolue, que, certes, n'est que ce qui est. Incontinent écarter cependant, sous un prétexte, le leurre, accuserait notre inconséquence, niant le plaisir que nous voulons prendre : car cet *au-delà* en est l'agent, et le moteur dirais-je si je ne répugnais à opérer, en public, le démontage impie de la fiction et conséquemment du mécanisme littéraire, pour étaler la pièce principale ou rien. Mais, je vénère comment, par une supercherie, on projette, à quelque élévation défendue et de foudre ! le conscient manque chez nous de ce qui là-haut éclate.

A quoi sert cela —

A un jeu.

En vue qu'une attirance supérieure comme d'un vide, nous avons droit, le tirant de nous par de l'ennui à l'égard des choses, si elles s'établissaient solides et préponderantes — éperdument les détache jusqu'à s'en remplir et aussi les douer de resplendissements, à travers l'espace vacant, en des fêtes à volonté et solitaires.

Quant à moi, je ne demande pas moins à l'écriture et vais prouver ce postulat.

La Nature a lieu, on n'y ajoutera pas ; que des cités, les voies ferrées et plusieurs inventions forment notre matériel.

Tout l'acte disponible, à jamais et seulement, reste de saisir les rapports, entre temps, rares ou multipliés ; d'après quelque état intérieur et que l'on veuille à son gré étendre, simplifier le monde.

A l'égal de créer : la notion d'un objet, échappant, qui fait défaut." [1]

[1] From *La Musique et les Lettres*.

Slaves of an absolute formula, we know assuredly that nothing exists save what exists. Under some pretext, however, to brush aside the lure would accuse our inconsequence, a negation of the pleasure we wish to have : for that *beyond* is the agent and I would add, the motor, were it not that I felt a distaste for taking to pieces impiously and in public the fiction and in consequence the mechanism of literature, in order to display the principal component or nothing. But I marvel how, by a deliberate ruse, one projects,

To this exposition of the process may be added one other remark of Mallarmé's :—

" À quoi bon la merveille de transposer un fait de nature en sa presque disparition vibratoire selon le jeu de la parole, cependant ; si ce n'est pour qu'en émane, sans la gêne d'un proche ou concret rappel, la notion pure." [1]

Both these quotations bring us back to the primary elements of poetry, a mind and words. The mind has at its disposal the two systems that make up words, sound-look and reference ; but here, in contrast to the everything-universe, the mind's attention must be drawn away from reference, because reference is experience, i.e. things, and the aim is no thing. So the attention must be shifted to the only other possibility, sound-look, and to the organization of the latter into a particular sort of system by which the mind might be deflected and enmeshed in a web of sound-look, and thus forget to attach to the groups of sounds and letters the things of experience linked to them by reference. And so those things of experience will disappear. The mind will find itself suspended momentarily in a tissue of sound—suspended over emptiness. To achieve this object the sound-look relation system will have to be constructed with extreme care, a system of nearly disembodied relations, working by necessity and not by chance, where the sound

to a height forbidden and lightning-haunted, the conscious lack in ourselves of that which bursts forth up there.

Of what use is that—

For a game.

A higher attraction, as of a void (which we draw from ourselves, as we have a right to do, through boredom with things if these were to establish themselves solidly and in the mastery) detaches them passionately until it can fill itself with them and also endow them with splendours, across vacant space, in deliberate and solitary festivals.

As for me, I ask no less than this of writing, and am going to prove this postulate.

Nature exists, there is no adding to it ; that cities, railways, and many inventions form our material.

All the action at one's disposal, eternally and solely, is to grasp the relationships, in the interval, rare or multiplied ; according to some interior state that one would like to extend at will, to simplify the world.

The equivalent of creation : the notion of an object that escapes, that is lacking.

[1] From *Divagations*, Crise de Vers. (Of what use the wonder of transposing a fact of nature into its near-disappearance in vibration according to the play of the word, however, if there were not to emanate from it, without the embarrassment of a near or concrete recalling, the pure idea.)

and the look of words will serve, not as chance producers of images of experience, but as the necessary principles in the construction of a system. The mind will sit and spin like a spider a system of pure relations, as Mallarmé says, "J'ai voulu te dire simplement que je venais de jeter le plan de mon Oeuvre entier, après avoir trouvé la clef de moi-même, clef de voûte, ou centre, si tu veux, pour ne pas nous brouiller de métaphores, — centre de moi-même, où je me tiens comme une araignée sacrée, sur les principaux fils déjà sortis de mon esprit, et à l'aide desquels je tisserai *aux points de rencontre* de merveilleuses dentelles, que je devine, et qui existent déjà dans le sein de la Beauté." [1]

But this also, as with the previous universe, is nothing strange to the mind. For this is logic, "the science of Relation in the abstract—of absolute Relation—of Relation considered solely in itself" (Poe, *Eureka*). This attempt therefore to construct a nothingness turns out to be an attempt to create a logic, just as the attempt to create an everythingness turned out to be an attempt to create a nightmare.

We are now getting to the stage where we shall know what to look for in the work of these two poets. Rimbaud, a mind trying to create an all-inclusive poetry universe, must concentrate on the reference aspect of language, attach words to experience as closely as possible to start with, multiply all possible relations between the references called up by words, and create ultimately a world inside which everything has of necessity significance, i.e. the world of nightmare. Mallarmé, a mind trying to create an all-exclusive poetry universe, must concentrate on sound-look, distract the mind from reference and experience by organizing a complex of relations of the sound-look aspect of language, and create ultimately a world in which the sound and look of the words make a perfect relation system without reference to anything, i.e. a world of logic.

[1] *Propos sur la Poésie*, letter to Théodore Aubanel, 28th July, 1866, pp. 70–1. I only wanted to tell you that I have just outlined the plan of my complete Work, after having found the key to myself, the keystone, or the centre if you like, so as not to mix our metaphors, the centre of myself, where I hold myself like a sacred spider, upon the principal threads already spun out of my mind, with the help of which I shall weave at the *points of intersection* wonderful lace-work which I guess at and which exists already at the heart of Beauty.

Once again one is struck by the looking-glass similarities between these two extremes. The construction of each of these two universes, everythingness and nothingness, turns on form. In each case the medium or elements employed, words, end up by being used not as significant in themselves but as drawing their significance from their position in the whole system, employed as positional symbols in a system of formal relations, in the one case a system of references, in the other a system of sound-look. Carnap, in *The Logical Syntax of Language* (p. 12), says, "A language which is concerned with the objects of any domain may designate these objects either by *proper names* or by systematic positional *co-ordinates*, that is by symbols which show the place of the objects in the system, and, thereby, their positions in relation to one another." This is so here. In the one case we have a system of purely formal relations between the references of words, so that nightmare may be attained where there is an independent all-inclusive system of images without words—and we have Rimbaud saying, "*Je ne sais plus parler*."[1] In the other case, we have a system of purely formal relations between sound-look, without reference to experience, as in logic—and we have Mallarmé saying, "J'ai presque perdu la raison et le sens des paroles les plus familières."[2]

If, therefore, at the start, the task these two had set themselves seemed nonsense to the rational mind, the latter was wrong. Impossibility would be consoling; it is the possibility of success that is so disturbing, as these two discovered. For the one sits like God in the six days of creation, making a universe, "I tried to invent new flowers, new stars, new flesh, new languages. I thought to acquire supernatural powers"[3]; and the other sits like God before whose face the earth and heaven fled away, contemplating infinite emptiness, "le Rien qui est la vérité,"[4] the Nothingness which is truth. It is not the impossibility of the attempt but the possibilities of success, glimpsed if nothing more,

[1] From Matin, *Une Saison en Enfer*. (I do not know how to speak any more.)
[2] *Propos sur la Poésie*, p. 82. (I have almost lost my reason and the sense of the most familiar words.)
[3] From Adieu, *Une Saison en Enfer*.
[4] *Propos sur la Poésie*, letter to Henri Cazalis, March, 1866, p. 59.

14. Rimbaud and the World of *Les Illuminations*

COLERIDGE, in his *Biographia Literaria*, says, " I learnt from him, that Poetry, even that of the loftiest and, seemingly, that of the wildest odes, had a logic of its own, as severe as that of science ; and more difficult, because more subtle, more complex, and dependent on more fugitive causes. In the truly great poets . . . there is a reason assignable, not only for every word, but for the position of every word." [1] This is not the attitude normally adopted towards Rimbaud by his critics. Rickword speaks of Rimbaud's " disuse of logic " [2] ; Ruchon says, " Let us not look for intellectual content in the *Illuminations*, particularly the prose ones. . . . He mixes up times and places, and laughs at categories of thought." [3] Dr. Starkie says of these same prose poems, " In the latter he wrote, as it were, automatically, without logical control, allowing the impressions to settle on him from without or to seep up from within, from the dark and troubled depths of his nature." [4]

In one sense this is fair enough. One reading of the *Illuminations* will convince the mind that they are not likely to prove tractable material to logical analysis. One might as well try to bring logic to bear on the traditional ballad :—

> " The lily, the rose, the rose I lay.
> And through the glass window shines the sun.
> How should I love and I so young ?
> The bailey beareth the bell away."

[1] S. T. Coleridge, *Biographia Literaria*, vol. i. Edited with his æsthetical essays by J. Shawcross, Clarendon Press, Oxford, 1907, ch. i, p. 4.
[2] Op. cit., ch. xv, p. 152.
[3] Francois Ruchon, *Jean-Arthur Rimbaud* : Sa Vie, Son Oeuvre, Son Influence, Librairie Ancienne Honoré Champion Editeur, Paris, 1929, ch. iii, pp. 128 and 138.
[4] Dr. Enid Starkie, *Arthur Rimbaud*, Hamish Hamilton, London, 1947, New and Revised Edition, ch. vi, p. 214.

Rimbaud abandoned the normal relations of logic—that is plain enough. But from this there results in the critics a curiously negative attitude, as if with logic had gone all hope of establishing any principle of connectedness in Rimbaud's work, so that any intellectual investigation would be unprofitable, almost impertinent. Dr. Starkie, for instance, quotes a passage from one of the *Illuminations*, and then says, " The literary critic would only destroy the poet's effect if he tried ponderously to comment on the passages. All Rimbaud's efforts have gone to prevent the control and the comment of his own rational mind and that of the pompous critic would be no more welcome." [1] Looking through these eyes we are confronted with the unsatisfactory prospect of a world of random chaos.

This point of view supposes that there is only one way of ordering material in the mind ; but in the course of this inquiry an alternative form of organization has come to light. This led in the last chapter to a description of a possible universe that could be built up by the mind on this other principle, that of dream-construction, a world of everythingness. In a hypothetical kind of poetry built on this system, none of the images would be random ones and none of the connections between the images would be without significance. This has now to be investigated.

Results so far point strongly to there being method in this madness. Rimbaud himself says in one of these poems, " Ma sagesse est aussi dédaignée que le chaos " (*Vies I*) (my wisdom is as much scorned as is chaos) ; but the investigation of a " sagesse " that couples itself with chaos is obviously going to be tricky, and will probably require unorthodox technique. In fact, if the inquiry is concerned with the method in madness, then the method of the inquiry may have to be mad too. It is therefore essential to be clear at this stage about the nature of the inquiry and the extent of the subject-matter.

The particular material here is the prose poems of the *Illuminations*.[2] These constitute the world to be explored,

[1] Op. cit., ch. vi, p. 219.

[2] For details about editions and dates of composition of these poems, see Dr. Starkie's chapter on *Les Illuminations* in *Arthur Rimbaud*.

and the aim is to discover the nature of the relations obtaining in it. Since these are poems, it is a world of words. We have already certain clues to work on: the suggestion that this is a world where the mind is directed away from the sound-look system of language towards the reference system; where the units are likely to be complex, with a maximum of relations between them; where the units themselves will draw their significance from their position in the system rather than from any inherent meaning they may be supposed to possess; lastly, where it may prove helpful to adopt the mental organization of Nightmare and Dream with its use of similarity and succession, rather than that of Logic and Number with *its* use of those same two principles.

Given, then, that the language organization of these poems is the scope of the inquiry, the next thing to be clear about is the part of that organization which will concern us. The point is that language, as has already been seen, is a double relationship system, and if we are to abandon one of these systems here as irrelevant and direct our attention wholly to the other, the reasons for this shift must first be clear. The shift in question is from the sound-look of language to reference. This is not necessarily an advantage, for it means that the attention has to grapple with a pattern of references and images in the mind instead of with such concrete things as syntax. But it seems plain that the shift so caused in the mind is deliberate on the poet's part. This may be something of what Rimbaud meant when he said in *Une Saison en Enfer*, "J'écrivais des silences."

There are four points to be noticed here. They are:—

(*a*) The use of normal vocabulary.
(*b*) The preponderance of words with direct reference to sense experience (those described in Chapter 4 under the heading "Stable word plus stabilized diversity of reference").
(*c*) The use of normal syntax.
(*d*) The adoption of the prose poem form instead of metrical or rhyming verse.

The normality of the vocabulary in these poems is

apparent even at a casual reading, the earlier mannerisms of the poet, such as the use of technical terms or of neologisms, having dropped away almost entirely. A few sentences taken at random will illustrate the type of vocabulary used.

" Oh ! le pavillon en viande saignante sur la soie des mers et des fleurs arctiques (elles n'existent pas)." (*Barbare.*)

" Le matin où, avec Elle, vous vous débattîtes parmi ces éclats de neige, ces lèvres vertes, ces glaces, ces drapeaux noirs et ces rayons bleus, et ces parfums pourpres du soleil des pôles. — Ta force." (*Metropolitain.*)

" Un coup de ton doigt sur le tambour décharge tous les sons et commence la nouvelle harmonie." (*À une Raison.*)

" Un bizarre dessin de ponts, ceux-ci droits, ceux-là bouclés, d'autres descendant en obliquant en angles sur les premiers ; et ces figures se renouvelant dans les autres circuits éclairés du canal, mais tous tellement longs et légers que les rives, chargées de dômes, s'abaissent et s'amoindrissent." [1] (*Ouvriers.*)

These examples will also give some idea of the frequent recurrence of what one might call experience-words (see (*b*) above). *Barbare*, the poem from which the first of them is taken, is one of the many *Illuminations* that consist almost entirely of words of this type. In some of the poems words of this kind mingle with words of the kind described in Chapter 4 under the heading " Stable word plus unstabilized diversity of reference "—abstract, in fact. These appear in varying proportions. Only very few of these poems, about five in all, are almost entirely abstract. *Guerre* is an example of this type :—

" Enfant, certains ciels ont affiné mon optique, tous les caractères nuancérent ma physionomie. Les phénomènes s'émurent.

[1] " Behold the pavilion of raw flesh set up on the silk of the seas and the Arctic flowers (which are not)."

" There was the morning when, with Her, you struggled amongst those banks of snow, those green-lipped crevasses, that ice, those black flags and blue rays, and the purple perfumes of the polar sun.—Thy force."

" One beat of your finger upon the drum sets loose all sounds, and is the birth of a new harmony."

" I see a strange design of bridges—some straight, some curved, others descending slantingly on to the first. They multiply themselves in the windings of the canal, but are so long and so light that the canal banks, covered with domes, seem to sink and grow less."

(Translations by Helen Rootham.)

" A présent, l'inflexion éternelle des moments de l'infini des mathématiques me chassent par ce monde où je subis tous les succès civils, respecté de l'enfance étrange et des affections énormes. Je songe à une guerre, de droit ou de force, de logique bien imprévue.

" C'est aussi simple qu'une phrase musicale." [1]

These abstract poems or sections of poems are by no means the least interesting of the collection, because they seem to be capable of acting as intelligible commentaries upon what is going on in the other poems.[2] But for that reason they can be postponed for the moment, since direct intelligibility will make them foreign to our purpose at this stage.

The examples so far given illustrate (*c*) above, the normality of the syntax. Ruchon says of this, " Rimbaud's syntax is perfectly clear, perfectly simple, in no way revolutionary." [3] Finally, we come to (*d*), the poet's use of the prose poem. Of the *Illuminations*, thirty-eight are prose-poems, two are in free verse, and eleven in some sort of metrical verse. We shall be concerned here only with that first big group.

These four characteristics of Rimbaud's work have the effect of shifting the attention from the sound-look system of language to the reference system. Everything is done to prevent the words drawing attention to themselves as such. They are ordinary words and individually they refer to ordinary experience ; their organization is normal, and there is no introduction of metre or rhyme to emphasize the sound-look organization. In Chapter 12 it was said that the normal organization of prose consists in words—syntax—sense. In the *Illuminations* Rimbaud, in the interests of his own particular brand of poetry, makes use of the

[1] WAR

When I was a child, certain skies refined my vision ; every kind of character helped to colour my face. Phenomena were moved. At present the eternal inflections of moments and the infinity of mathematics hunts me through this world where I endure every civil success, respected by a strange childhood and by great affections.

I dream of a war, of right or of force, of a quite unforeseen logic.

It is as simple as a musical phrase.

(Ibid.)

[2] Present evidence seems to suggest that they were written later than the others. See Dr. Starkie on this point.

[3] Op. cit., ch. v, p. 187.

fact, deplored by more precise types of mind, that it is perfectly possible to use normal words and normal syntax and to arrive at nonsense. The order of language is used to create the universe of disorder.

We now come to the main question, the relations in the reference system of Rimbaud's poetry. This is a fair sample, from *Phrases*, of the type of thing confronting us :—

" J'ai tendu des cordes de clocher à clocher ; des guirlandes de fenêtre à fenêtre ; des chaînes d'or d'étoile à étoile, et je danse.

Le haut étang fume continuellement. Quelle sorcière va se dresser sur le couchant blanc ? Quelles violettes frondaisons vont descendre ?

Pendant que les fonds publics s'écoulent en fêtes de fraternité, il sonne une cloche de feu rose dans les nuages." [1]

As has been said already, no normal logic holds this together. What other possibilities are there in the way of connecting threads ?

One may try to get help from the critics at this point. One after another formulates the problem. Mr. Day Lewis speaks of " that unifying force—the intensity of feeling which alone . . . can take the place of poetic reason in fusing together and controlling the images of pure perception " ; a little later he inquires " Can we define some active principle making for poetic association ? " [2] but any answer to the question is bogged in archetypes and " the eternal spirit's eternal pastime ". Mr. Richards says, " In this ' physical relativity ' words may be compared with colours, but of the laws governing the effects of collocation and admixture hardly anything is known " [3] ; in another work he suggests that metre is the unifying and controlling force

[1] " I have hung ropes from bell-tower to bell-tower ; garlands from window to window ; golden chains from star to star—and I dance.

A vapour eddies up continually from the mere. What sorceress will rise up against the white sunset ? What fretted violet shapes will descend ?

While the public funds are being spent in festivals of brotherhood, a bell of rosy fire rings up in the clouds."

(Translation by Helen Rootham.)

[2] *The Poetic Image*, ch. v, pp. 133 and 146.

[3] I. A. Richards, *Practical Criticism* : A Study of Literary Judgment, Kegan Paul, Trench, Trubner, and Co., Ltd., London, 1929, pt. iii, ch. iii, p. 213.

in poetry [1]; but that cannot help us here. Caudwell falls back upon the unity of the ego: "Poetry is a relationship of memory-images, mediated by only two words—'I' and 'Like'," [2] upon the social relations between one mind and another, and upon the "affective cord" linking images together, i.e. emotion again. Coleridge suggests other possibilities, and is more helpful; he says of images, "They become proofs of original genius only as far as they are modified by a predominant passion; or by associated thoughts or images awakened by that passion; or when they have the effect of reducing multitude to unity, or succession to an instant." [3]

Apart from Coleridge's last sentence, none of these seem to offer the necessary guiding thread through this labyrinth. The difficulty is that we are inside a mind, so to speak, which we have to explore, or rather, not inside one mind but two, the poet's and the reader's. The world of the poem is going to be made up of relations between images in those two minds; but the poet cannot fully control the chance associations that his poem will arouse among the memory-images of his reader, while equally the reader cannot hope wholly to fathom the private mind of the poet. Between the two, the product of each mind, is the poem. There are admittedly other ways of gaining admission to another's mind, and we might find the poet storming the reader's mind by imparting his own emotion, or the reader forcing admission to the poet's mind by a psycho-analytical interpretation of the images used. But neither of these methods seems to have much to do with poetry. So for the moment let us come to the common ground between the two minds, the poem. Any prose poem of the *Illuminations* will be a world to which I shall be admitted by reading it. It will be partly Rimbaud's, in so far as the making of it in words was his, and partly mine, in so far as his words and images and references will call up other arbitrary words and images and references in my mind. But out of Rimbaud's images and mine (or those of any other reader)

[1] *Principles of Literary Criticism*, ch. xxiv, p. 192 *et seq.*
[2] *Illusion and Reality*, ch. x, p. 208.
[3] *Biographia Literaria*, vol. ii, ch. xv, p. 16.

it may be possible to construct some sort of world which will hold together. At any rate, the experiment seems worth making.

The first step is to allow one's mind to produce its own related images as it goes through a Rimbaud poem ; these should be written down as they appear, and then it can be seen whether any kind of constructional unity holds the sum-total together. This is a very unorthodox way of going to work, but some other method than a logical one has obviously got to be tried, and in point of fact, it is not as dangerous as it appears. The resulting network of personal images allied to those of the poem will not claim in any way to be an interpretation, still less *the* interpretation, of the poem. It need be regarded as nothing more than a way into this world, and indeed for me the only way in, since one can make experiments only with one's own mind. But more important still, it has to be borne in mind that what is being investigated is a relation system, a structure, a way of holding things together ; and what the elements consist of in such a system is irrelevant. It is like Lewis Carroll building up sound exercises in logic with such elements as hedgehogs reading *The Times*. The elements do not matter in themselves ; but they have got to be there. Even the most rarefied treatise on Symbolic Logic makes use of hieroglyphics on a page to give its relations something to bite on, so to speak. The following experiments or exercises may be thought of in the same way. (Translations of poems in Figs. 2–7 will be found in the Appendix, Figs. 3 and 4 at end of book.)

15. Rimbaud and The World of *Les Illuminations (continued)*

" How are phantasies created? From the poets we learn much about it; from science little." (Jung.)

IN the preceding chapter, four lines of investigation of the world of *Les Illuminations* were suggested. The first, the question whether in this world the mind was distracted from the sound-look of language to reference, has already been dealt with. The remaining three were briefly as follows: Is this a world (*a*) where the units draw significance from their position in the system rather than from any intrinsic meaning they may be supposed to possess? (*b*) where the units are complex, with a maximum of relations between them? (*c*) where the mental organization of Dream and Nightmare, rather than that of Number and Logic, is the principle of construction? These problems must now be considered in the light of the experiments set out in Figs. 2–4.

First, then, question (*a*). Freud, speaking of an attempt to reconstruct a dream, says, " If the procedure is exercised on oneself, the best plan of helping the experiment is to write down at once all one's first indistinct fancies. . . . We especially direct our attention to the *unbidden* associations *which disturb our thoughts*—those which are otherwise put aside by the critic as worthless refuse." [1] As far as my own experiments are concerned, I make haste to forestall the said critic, partly for safety's sake, but mainly because, strangely enough, the fact that the units on my side of the dream world are worthless in themselves is capital to the argument. Of course, the individual and personal associations of any mind in connection with any of the *Illuminations*

[1] *On Dreams*, p. 9. (I have reversed the order of the two remarks.)

are worthless as such. This point was already mentioned at the end of Chapter 14, but it cannot be too strongly emphasized, because Figs. 2–4 are not to be regarded as interpretations of the poems concerned. They are only ways of thinking, just as Fig. 1. was a way of thinking. The elements do not matter except in so far as they are " points de rencontre ", as Mallarmé says, nodal points for relationships. The elements could be entirely different. Another mind than mine would produce a totally different set of associated images, but whatever came along, cream meringues or railway engines or orange and white guinea pigs, it would not matter in the least. My personal associations may, I trust, be regarded as being without significance. For that will leave us free to examine the really significant thing, the relations of the system.

The next point is (*b*), the number and complexity of the relations uniting the units. Here the diagrams may speak for themselves. Indeed, anyone attempting a similar experiment will find that when once the units of the double poem-world are set out, the difficulty is not that there are too few relations but that there are almost too many. The idea-threads, as I have called them, are not important for their content, only as showing a principle of connectedness ; and the ones listed are not the only possible ones. Obvious ones, such as colour connections, have been left out. So, too, in Fig. 4 there is a possible idea-thread of Smallness, the animals being lesser animals, the flowers tiny and near the ground, the child itself dwarfed by the village square, by the steeples and the sky. There is another also, suggesting an affinity between animals and human beings. In Fig. 3 there is an idea-thread to do with pillars—cords, rods, pillars, foxgloves, sceptres ; and another connecting sun and sky and water. These and others were not included because it would have been possible to go on indefinitely, and there were enough already to demonstrate the multiplicity of the relations and the complex nature of the units. (Compare the word " rose-nobles " in Fig. 3, for instance.) It is worth remembering Freud's remark that all dream content is over-determined.[1]—" There will be found no factor in the

[1] *On Dreams*, p. 43.

dream whence the chain of associations does not lead in two or more directions, no scene which has not been pieced together out of two or more impressions." [1]

The position at this stage is a paradoxical one. The associated ideas and images in this poem-world are unimportant and could be other—that is, they are irrelevant. But binding them all together is a network of double and triple relations, so that none of the ideas *appears* irrelevant. How can things be relevant and irrelevant at one and the same time? Or to put the question a little differently, can the mind be in a state where it will accept as relevant any idea or image that turns up *by chance*?

And behind this comes a bigger question still, brought in by the mention of chance. The associated images in the poem-world are inevitably chance, the product of hazard in the mind of the chance reader, uncontrollable by the poet. How then can this poem-world be art if it is ruled by chance? Many of the critics quoted earlier seem to accept the rôle of chance in this poetry, as if Rimbaud wrote at hazard and could be read so. I am not prepared to accept this view. Rimbaud himself seems to deny it in that strange and interesting remark in *Vies I*, which almost suggests that he could, in fact, control the resources of another's mind: "Je vous indiquerais les richesses inouîes. J'observe l'histoire des trésors que vous trouvâtes. Je vois la suite!" [2] Whatever art may be, it is not the product of Chance. Valéry repeats this theme over and over again: "To remove oneself from the arbitrary; to shut oneself off from the accidental." [3] So does Mallarmé, who speaks of "chance overcome word by word". If the world of the *Illuminations* is the product of chance, then there is no more to be said, and no investigation of it is possible. But in that case it is not art, or poetry. Provided one is prepared to say that it is poetry, it must follow that there is some principle of construction. Chance could assemble the elements, but it could not build a system because a system

[1] Ibid., pp. 34–5.

[2] "I could point out unheard-of riches to you. I know the history of the treasures you have found. I see the sequel!"

(Translation by Helen Rootham.)

[3] *Mélange*, p. 34.

or order is the negation of chance. What in these poem-worlds is the principle that unites the chance elements and by so uniting them makes them cease to be chance?

It needs to be made clear once again that all this happens in the mind. The notions of relevance and irrelevance, as also those of chance and necessity, are in the mind, and it is there that we must look for an answer to this problem. The question may be more precisely formulated as follows: How can the poet by his poem induce in the reader's mind a condition such that any chance associated image will be accepted and incorporated in the relation-system set up in that mind by the poem? In short, how can chance become necessity?

There is a remark in Valéry which provides a clue to the answer. It is this: "But how can the work be insured against the vicissitudes of thought, and how fortified against the sensation of the arbitrary? By arbitrary chance itself, by chance organized and brought under control." [1] It sounds strange to talk of a state of mind where chance might deliberately be taken as necessity, but we have met it before, for Fig. 1 makes it plain that this is the progress out of the field of Language which is also the field of probability (i.e. subject to chance) towards Dream and Nightmare. This brings us to the still outstanding question, (*c*), whether the world of the *Illuminations* may be constructed according to the principles of Dream and Nightmare rather than those of Number and Logic.

It should be clear by now that the world of the *Illuminations* is in the mind, and that the mind is in a particular state where it creates a complex system out of all the chance material offered to it. The first thing that needs to be established is that this state of mind is the state of dream, and this can be done without difficulty. First, the material of the dreaming mind is the product of hazard. Any dreamer knows how the mind in dream picks up chance sights and speeches of the day, old memories, fantastic words and names accidentally heard—in fact, any old thing in the memory, on which to work. I am not here concerned with the Freudian theory of iron determinism in the choice

[1] *Variété IV*, p. 45.

of dream-images, resulting from the workings of the subconscious mind. The latter falls outside my terms of reference. My point is simply that the store of memories which the mind has at its disposal for dream-construction is the product of chance, the sum-total of all the accidental happenings and experiences of a being in an apparently random world. Secondly, the dreaming mind builds up its chance material into a multiple and complex system. " One can at least go far enough to become convinced that the dream is an ingenious construction," [1] as Freud says. Thirdly, the dreaming mind accepts everything offered to it by chance, by memory, by external circumstances which affect the sleeper's body, such as noises, by the inner and outer sensations of the body itself. Valéry says of it, " Nightmare knits up into an all-powerful drama a certain diversity of independent sensations that works upon us in sleep," [2] and adds, " In dreams everything is automatically included, nothing left out."

It can be seen now that the poem-world of the *Illuminations* and the world of dream coincide so exactly in the mind that they must be one and the same. The world of these poems is the world of Dream and Nightmare. How does this come about?

We have to discover how Rimbaud puts his reader into this state. Dr. Starkie, in the passages quoted in the preceding chapter, suggests that he does it by dreaming himself, communicating his mental state of inattention as if it were catching, like a fit of yawning. But this seems hardly possible. To put another mind into a state of dream, something more active is required in the agent than to be in that state himself. The communication of dreams is a certain way to bore people, i.e. to send them to sleep, which is perhaps one way of inducing a state of dream in another mind, but not presumably what a poet would want to do. Valéry hits the nail on the head when he says, " It is not by inattention and dreaming that one imposes upon words such rare and precious adjustments. The true condition of a true poet is that which is most distinct in the

[1] *The Interpretation of Dreams*, ch. vii, p. 415.
[2] *Variété II*, p. 251.

state of dreaming. . . . Indeed, anyone wishing to write down his dream owes it to himself to be infinitely awake." [1] If the process of setting another mind in a state of dream is not an affair of hazard, the means of doing it should be discoverable. And since Rimbaud is a poet, the means here must be words and a way of using them.

Certain characteristics of Rimbaud's use of words have already been discussed. There remains one, however, which is of first importance. This is concentration. "Concentration of imagery" is a phrase which can be used very glibly in literary criticism. It will be advisable, therefore, to examine here exactly what meaning may be ascribed to it. The quotations already given in the text and in Figs. 2–4 will illustrate what is meant, the way Rimbaud packs his images as tightly in a sentence as possible, so that even a short sentence or phrase will contain as many image-producing words as possible. A few more instances of this kind of thing may be helpful :—

"Au-dessus du niveau des plus hautes crêtes une mer troublée par la naissance éternelle de Vénus, chargée de flottes orphéoniques et de la rumeur des perles et des conques précieuses, la mer s'assombrit parfois avec des éclats mortels. Sur les versants, des moissons de fleurs grandes comme nos armes et nos coupes mugissent. Des cortèges de Mabs en robes rousses, opalines, montent des ravines. Là-haut, les pieds dans la cascade et les ronces, les cerfs tettent Diane. Les Bacchantes des banlieues sanglottent et la lune brûle et hurle. Vénus entre dans les cavernes des forgerons et des ermites. Des groupes de beffrois chantent les idées des peuples. Des châteaux bâtis en os sort la musique inconnue."

"Devant une neige, un Être de beauté de haute taille. Des sifflements de mort et des cercles de musique sourde font monter, s'élargir et trembler comme un spectre ce corps adoré ; des blessures écarlates et noires éclatent dans les chairs superbes."

"Les prés remontent aux hameaux sans coqs, sans enclumes. L'écluse est levée. Ô les calvaires et les moulins de désert, les îles et les meules !

Des fleurs magiques bourdonnaient. Les talus le berçaient. Des bêtes d'une élégance fabuleuse circulaient. Les nuées

[1] *Variété I*, p. 56.

s'amassaient sur la haute mer faite d'une éternité de chaudes larmes."

MARINE

Les chars d'argent et de cuivre,
Les proues d'acier et d'argent
Battent l'écume,
Soulèvent les souches des ronces.
Les courants de la lande
Et les ornières immenses du reflux
Filent circulairement vers l'est,
Vers les piliers de la forêt,
Vers les fûts de la jetée,
Dont l'angle est heurté par des tourbillons de lumière.[1]

It is, I believe, this characteristic of extreme concentration in Rimbaud's poetry which causes his critics to contradict one another so. " One could claim that the poet deliberately suppresses the verbs to lighten the sentence and give more

[1] These extracts are from *Villes I* (which is perhaps the most sustained example of concentration in the *Illuminations*), *Being Beauteous*, and *Enfance II*.

" Above the level of the highest crests is a sea troubled by the eternal birth of Venus, and covered with choric fleets and the distant murmurs of pearls and rare sinuous shells. Sometimes the sea grows dark with mortal thunders. On the slopes there bellow harvests of flowers as big as our goblets. Corteges of Queen Mabs in robes red and opaline, climb the ravines. Up there, their hoofs in the cascades and the briars, the stags give Diana suck. Bacchantes of the suburbs weep, and the moon burns and howls. Venus enters the caves of the blacksmiths and hermits. Groups of bell-towers sing aloud the ideas of the people. From castles built of bones proceeds unknown music."

" Against a background of snow is a beautiful Being of majestic stature. Death is all round her, and whistling, dying breaths, and circles of hollow music, cause this adored body to rise, to swell, and to tremble like a spectre. Scarlet and black wounds break out on the superb flesh."

" The fields slope up to the villages, left empty of cocks and anvils. The sluices are open. Oh ! The Calvaries and the windmills in the desert, the islands and the hayricks.

Magic flowers hummed all around. The gentle slopes lulled them to rest. Beasts of a fabulous elegance walked about. Far beyond, over the sea—that eternity of hot tears—clouds massed themselves."

Chariots of silver and of copper
Prows of steel and of silver
Beat the foam
Lift the stems of the brambles.
The streams of the barren parts
And the immense tracks of the ebb
Flow circularly towards the east,
Towards the pillars of the forest,
Towards the piles of the jetty,
Against whose angles are hurled whirlpools of light.

(Translations by Helen Rootham.)

of a lift to his thought "[1]; "The imagery with Rimbaud . . . always envisages reality under the appearance of mobility; that is to say, the verb plays a preponderant rôle in it."[2] "Poetry such as this leaves the reader infinitely more free when confronted with it than classical or romantic poetry "[3]; "This poetry is in danger of shutting out by the finality of his descriptions that loop-hole for rêverie. . . ."[4] The muddle is understandable, because such extreme concentration, and hence the things that result from it, are rare in poetry. I know of only one other poet who approaches it, the writer of lines such as :—

> " . . . Time, milk and magic, from the world beginning.
> Time is the tune my ladies lend their heartbreak,
> From bald pavilions and the house of bread
> Time tracks the sound of shape on man and cloud,
> On rose and icicle the ringing handprint."[5]

In fact, the images are so closely packed that something happens to the mind that is taking them in, and this something has to do with the shifting of the mind out of the field of experience. The elements, the mental images of experience, remain unchanged, but the mind is compelled to organize them differently. This difference is going to lie in the use made of the principles of similarity and succession, a use opposite to that made in Number and Logic.

Let us take succession first.

However concentrated a succession of images may be, it cannot alter the fact that the mind is in general subject to time.[6] Any succession of words bringing with them their attendant succession of images must go along one by one. Concentration in poetry cannot mean that the words as sound-look are concentrated or concertina-ed. It is only in Jabberwocky, in nonsense and laughter, that it is possible to make " mimsy " from " flimsy and miserable ". But

[1] Hackett, op. cit., ch. vii, p. 166, footnote.
[2] Ruchon, op. cit., p. 184.
[3] Daniel-Rops, *Rimbaud : Le Drama Spirituel*, Librairie Plon, Paris, 1936, ch. viii, p. 174.
[4] Rickword, op. cit., ch. xiii, p. 138.
[5] From *Twenty-Five Poems*, by Dylan Thomas.
[6] Cf. Bridgman, op. cit., p. 11, " All mental operations must be made in time, and are therefore ordered in time."

images in the mind, the reference side of language, need not follow so rigid a 1, 2, 3, 4 succession in time.[1] Suppose the image-bringing words to be concentrated in the closest possible succession—then the mind might give up the attempt to keep the images separate. This is the abandonment of the organization of Number. Rimbaud's remark, "Les hallucinations sont innombrables" [2] (hallucinations are innumerable), could be taken in more senses than one. The simplest form of this instinctive classification of external reality is, of course, numerical—mathematics. "The most elementary act of self-consciousness is that which separates the 'I' from Nature, and this recognition of separation, of discontinuity, when sympathetically introjected into objects, makes possible the conception of numerous things." [3] Where, to put the matter very simply, one cannot go along counting one, two, three, four, where everything has become one, succession vanishes, because a series can only exist where there are a number of terms. Where all the terms have become one, "if all the trees were one tree," in fact, a series is not possible.[4] It is a state that would be like trying to play billiards with balls made of quicksilver. In Rimbaud this is exactly what happens. Everything is there all at once : "Les voix reconstituées ; l'éveil fraternel de toutes les énergies chorales et orchestrales et leurs applications instantanées, l'occasion, unique, de dégager nos sens." [5] "Arrivée de toujours, tu t'en iras partout." [6]

[1] Cf. J. W. Dunne, *An Experiment with Time*, A. and C. Black, Ltd., London, 1927, pt. iii, ch. viii, p. 54 : "The associational network stretched, not merely this way and that way in Space, but also backwards and forwards in Time ; and the dreamer's attention, following in natural, unhindered fashion the easiest pathway across the ramifications, would be continually crossing and recrossing that properly non-existent equator which we, waking, ruled quite arbitrarily athwart the whole."

[2] From *Une Saison en Enfer*, Nuit de l'Enfer.

[3] Caudwell, op. cit., ch. viii, p. 148.

[4] Cf. Dunne, op. cit., pt. v, ch. xx, p. 123 : "A 'Series' is a collection of individually distinguishable items arranged, or considered as arranged, in a sequence determined by some sort of ascertainable law."

[5] From *Solde*.
"Reconstituted voices : the brotherly awakening of all choral and orchestral energies, and their instantaneous application ! A unique opportunity to redeem our senses !"

[6] From *À Une Raison*.
"For ever arriving, everywhere you will pass away."

(Translations by Helen Rootham.)

It must now be obvious that the same thing is going to happen with similarity. It, too, depends upon things being separate, upon the notion of Number—two, three, four, or more things that may be compared because they are separate. If everything becomes one and the same, the notion of similarity vanishes in identification. The last poem quoted from the *Illuminations*, " Marine " shows this well; in it the land is not compared to the sea, it has become the sea, and the sea the land. It is a world where a house does not resemble its owner, it *is* its owner, so that if the house is the March Hare's, the chimneys are ears and the roof is thatched with fur.

Wittgenstein says, " Roughly speaking, to say of *two* things that they are identical is nonsense, and to say of *one* thing that it is identical with itself is to say nothing."[1] That is true, but the nonsense of the first half may be poetry. To say " You are yourself " is to say nothing; but to say,

> " Tree you are,
> Moss you are,
> You are violets with wind above them,"

may be poetry.[2] It is worth noticing also that the abandonment of the idea of Number and separateness means also the abandonment of " Number 1 ", if I may be forgiven the vulgarity, i.e. of the self. This is pointed out in the quotation from Caudwell given earlier. Now at last it is understandable that Rimbaud should say " Je est *un autre* " or " Enfin, ô bonheur, ô raison, j'écartai du ciel l'azur, qui est du noir, et je vécus, étincelle d'or de la lumière *nature* ".[3] The abandonment of the self as a separate entity and hence its identification with its surroundings, is met with in much other poetry. The loss of self may be partial, in which case we are in the world of Dream :—

> " And the stars came and set within my eyes,
> And snowy clouds rested upon my shoulders,
> And the blue sky shimmered deep within me " . . .

[1] Op. cit., p. 139, 5.5303.
[2] From *A Girl*, by Ezra Pound.
[3] From the *Lettre du Voyant* and *Une Saison en Enfer*, Alchimie du Verbe. (At length, o joy, o reason, I pushed back from the sky its blueness, which is darkness, and I lived, a spark of gold of the light, *Nature*.)

or it may be total :—

"I have lain on the floor of the sea and breathed with the breathing of the sea-anemone" . . . [1]

and here, as the context makes very plain, it is Nightmare, the terror that lies in the conviction, "This is none of I."

If to abandon the sense of separateness in the mind is to abandon the sense of Number, it is also to abandon one of the particular functions of language. As we saw in Chapter 4, it is one of the primary purposes of language to provide, in its words, small separate units for the mind to manipulate, convenient packets of experience which the mind can manage where it could not manage the chaotic multiplicity of total experience. So in Rimbaud this function of the sound-look of words is thwarted or suppressed by the concentration of the references. "Je suis maître du silence," [2] I am the lord of silence.

Coleridge, in the second passage from *Biographia Literaria*, quoted in Chapter 14, says that images may have the function of "reducing multitude to unity, or succession to an instant". This fits well here, for Rimbaud, by the closely packed images of the *Illuminations*, achieves that very thing, making the reader's mind discard its usual organization of words and images in small separate units, so that a new and far greater unity can be produced, a unity where everything in the cosmos runs into everything else in one enormous oneness, and in place of succession and similarity there only remain simultaneity in space-time, and identification. Miss Edith Sitwell makes this point when she says of the *Illuminations*, "This hallucination consists, to my mind, not so much in transforming actualities into other actualities, as in making all things as one, in abolishing time and place, in making all times as one, all places as one." [3] Rimbaud himself says, "I accustomed myself to simple hallucination : I saw quite openly a mosque in the place of a factory, a school of drums made by the angels, carriages on the

[1] The first of these two quotations is from *Ecstasy*, by W. J. Turner, the second from *Murder in the Cathedral*, by T. S. Eliot.

[2] From *Enfance V*.

[3] Introductory Essay to *Prose Poems from Les Illuminations of Arthur Rimbaud*, put into English by Helen Rootham, Faber and Faber, London, 1932, p. 44.

highways of the sky, a drawing-room at the bottom of a lake. . . . Then I explained my magic sophisms with the hallucination of words."[1] But psychologists maintain that hallucination and dream and nightmare are all the same. It is the state, literally, of "all at once", the "possession immédiate" of *Solde*. It explains the restlessness and mobility of the world of *Les Illuminations*, noted by Ruchon, which is a commonplace of dreams. It is, as everyone knows, impossible to hold a dream image clear and steady, as it is always changing. Writer after writer on dreams confirms this; "Our dreams are like dissolving views in which the dissolving process is carried on swiftly or slowly but always uninterruptedly"[2]; "From this come the absurd dreams where an object remains as it is and at the same time becomes something else."[3] "The whole picture is fluid, caught up in continuous change."[4] It also explains the absurdity of the compositions, judged from the standpoint of experience, compositions such as "On joue aux cartes au fond de l'étang",[5] (a game of cards is going on at the bottom of the pond). Freud, in his writings, keeps separate the two notions of condensation and displacement in the dream, but it seems probable that they both have this common cause, the abandonment of the relations of Number and Logic, and the merging of everything into one. The Duchess's baby, in *Alice in Wonderland*, is a good example, being at the same time a baby and a pig in one. Condensation and displacement are both there, but what matters is the oneness. The same thing is visible in this passage from *Une Saison en Enfer*, "À chaque être, plusieurs *autres vies* me semblaient dues. Ce monsieur ne sait ce qu'il fait : il est un ange. Cette famille est une nichée de chiens. Devant plusieurs hommes, je causai tout haut avec un

[1] From *Une Saison en Enfer*, Alchimie du Verbe. "Je m'habituai à l'hallucination simple : je voyais très franchement une mosquée à la place d'une usine, une école de tambours faite par des anges, des calèches sur les routes du ciel, un salon au fond d'un lac... Puis, j'expliquai mes sophismes magiques avec l'hallucination des mots !"

[2] Havelock Ellis, op. cit., p. 36.

[3] Henri Bergson, *Dreams*, translated by Edwin E. Slosson, T. Fisher Unwin, London, 1914, p. 57.

[4] Spitta, op. cit., ch. v, p. 168. See also Dunne, op. cit., ch. xxiii, p. 168.

[5] From *Soir Historique*.

moment d'une de leurs autres vies. — Ainsi, j'ai aimé un porc." [1] (Apparently somebody else besides the Duchess's baby had the misfortune to turn into a pig.)

Where the process is fully achieved, the world of the *Illuminations* is the world of Nightmare, a closed system, an inviolable unity which can absorb all disorder. The sense of similarity and succession has been suppressed, but with it has been suppressed its opposite, the sense of incongruity and incoherence. Once the poet has occasioned this state of mind in the reader, the latter is no longer in a position to reject any chance association of ideas as irrelevant and incoherent, and therefore will accept any idea as relevant and join it into the system ; so chance has become necessity. This is what we set out to prove.

By the operation of his poetry in the *Illuminations*, Rimbaud brings his reader into that condition which he terms, in the *Lettre du Voyant*, "la plénitude du grand songe," the fullness of dreaming *in excelsis*. But to do this is no work for a dreamer. This explanation of the principle on which the *Illuminations* are constructed lends a new significance to such words as " Le poète se fait *voyant* par un long, immense et raisonné *dérèglement* de *tous les sens* ", in the *Lettre du Voyant* (the poet makes himself a *seer* by a long, vast, and reasoned *disordering* of *all the senses*), a significance much more interesting than the usual explanation : that Rimbaud believed a life of moral debauchery was necessary to the true poet. So, too, with the remark, "Je finis par trouver sacré le désordre de mon esprit." [2] A cult of disorder would be a logical necessity in someone who was proposing to construct a world of Nightmare, but it would need to be deliberate, the work of somebody wide awake, as Rimbaud himself says :—

" — Mais je m'aperçois que mon esprit dort.

S'il était bien éveillé toujours à partir de ce moment, nous serions bientôt à la vérité, qui peut-être nous entoure avec ses

[1] From *Une Saison en Enfer*, Alchimie du Verbe. (To each individual, various *other lives* seemed to me to be due. This gentleman does not know what he is doing : he is an angel. This family is a litter of dogs. When faced with certain men, I have conversed out loud with a moment of one of their lives.— So, too, I loved a swine.)

[2] From *Une Saison en Enfer*, Alchimie du Verbe. (I ended up by regarding the disorder of my spirit as sacred.)

anges pleurants !... — S'il avait été éveillé jusqu'à ce moment-ci, c'est que je n'aurais pas cédé aux instincts délétères, à une époque immémoriale !... S'il avait toujours été bien éveillé, je voguerais en pleine sagesse ! " [1]

But the poet's intelligence has to produce Nightmare and not sense, disorder and not order. The moment the concentration of the images slackens, and the reader, as distinct from the poet, is allowed to wake up, the system ceases to be unified because the words cease to be the instrument of Nightmare, and the poem " deviates into sense ". Under this heading come those *Illuminations* mentioned earlier which are partly composed of concentrated imagery and partly of abstracts. Two examples follow :—

JEUNESSE

III

Les voix instinctives exilées... L'ingénuité physique amèrement rassise... Adagio. Ah ! l'égoisme infini de l'adolescence, l'optimisme studieux : que le monde était plein de fleurs cet été ! Les airs et les formes mourant... Un choeur, pour calmer l'impuissance et l'absence ! Un choeur de verres de mélodies nocturnes... En effet les nerfs vont vite chasser.[2]

VEILLÉES

II

L'éclairage revient à l'arbre de bâtisse. Des deux extrémités de la salle, décors quelconques, des élévations harmoniques se joignent. La muraille en face du veilleur est une succession psychologique de coupes, de frises, de bandes atmosphériques et d'accidents géologiques. — Rêve intense et rapide de groupes

[1] From *Une Saison en Enfer*, L'Impossible. (But I perceive that my mind is asleep. If it were always fully awake from this moment on, we should soon arrive at truth, who perhaps surrounds us with her weeping angels ! If it had always been awake up till this moment then I should not have given way to harmful instincts in an immemorial age ! If it had always been fully awake, I should be sailing along in full wisdom !)

[2] The voices which instructed us are exiled. . . . Physical ingenuousness is become bitterly sedate. . . . Adagio. Ah ! the infinite egoism of adolescence, studious optimism : how full was the world of flowers that summer ! The dying airs and shapes. . . . A choir to still helplessness and absence ! A choir of glasses, of nocturnal melodies. . . . It is true, our nerves will soon go a-hunting.

sentimentaux avec des êtres de tous les caractères parmi toutes les apparences.[1]

In the first of these two, certain of the phrases, the opening one, for instance, or " les airs et les formes mourant ", will induce the dreaming state, but in between come those other phrases such as " l'impuissance et l'absence ", as if they were commentaries and hence detached. This is an example of more abstract passages in the *Illuminations* seeming to act as comments upon the poetic process afoot in the work. It comes out even more clearly in the second of these two examples where the first half reads like dream poetry, whereas the second half states the characteristics of that world as we have discovered them, its dream nature, its condensation, its simultaneity and its all-embracing nature—but states them explicitly. Poems of this type hold the mind in a limbo between dream and intelligibility. In a few of the poems the dream element has gone completely, and the interest is solely in what is said, and in the light it throws on the nature of the other poems. I give one example :—

JEUNESSE

IV

Tu en es encore à la tentation d'Antoine. L'ébat du zèle écourté ; les tics d'orgueil puéril, l'affaissement et l'effroi. Mais tu te mettras à travail : toutes les possibilités harmoniques et architecturales s'émouvront autour de ton siège. Des êtres parfaits, imprévus, s'offriront à tes expériences. Dans tes environs affluera rêveusement la curiosité d'anciennes foules et de luxes oisifs. Ta mémoire et tes sens ne seront que la nourriture de ton impulsion créatrice. Quant au monde, quand tu sortiras, que sera-t-il devenu ? En tout cas, rien des apparences actuelles.[2]

[1] The light touches the shaft of the building. The decorations rise from floor to ceiling in a harmonious scale of colour. The wall in front of the watcher is a psychological succession of curves, friezes, atmospheric changes of light and shadow, and geological accidents. It is a vivid and rapid dream of sentimental groups, with all sorts of beings in all sorts of disguises.

(Translations by Helen Rootham.)

[2] Thou art, as yet, no further advanced than the temptation of Saint Anthony.

The sport of curtailed zeal, the habits of a puerile pride, despondency, and fright.

But thou wilt set thyself to this work : all harmonic and architectural possibilities will arise round thy seat. Beings who are perfect, unforeseen,

It is again an almost perfect commentary on what is attempted in the *Illuminations*. But for that very reason, and because the aim here is communication of an intelligible order, we seem to have passed out of poetry into prose.

The process works only where the chaos is complete; and so we come back to the words of Rimbaud quoted earlier, " Ma sagesse est aussi dédaignée que le chaos." It is clear now that the " sagesse " *is* chaos, of deliberate choice and construction, an infinity of everythingness in total disorder. But there is a second half to that remark which is very much to the point here. In full, it runs like this : " Ma sagesse est aussi dedaignée que le chaos. Qu'est mon néant, auprès de la stupeur qui vous attend ? " [1] " Sagesse " in the poet, " stupeur " in the reader, and between them chaos—no more perfect definition of the world of *Les Illuminations* could have been produced.

It was said earlier that it was by oneness that this world of Nightmare, of disorder, of everythingness, existed. A logician says, " Here the respective interpretations of the symbols 0 and 1 in the system of Logic are *Nothing* and *Universe*." [2] In our own particular system we have dealt with 1, or the Universe, or Rimbaud. There now remains 0, Nothing,—Mallarmé.

will offer themselves to thy experience. In thy neighbourhood the curiosity of ancient crowds and idle luxuries will flow dreamily. Thy memory and thy senses will be only the nourishment of thy creative impulse. As to the world, when thou comest out, what will it have become? In any case, there will be nothing left of its present appearances.

(Translation by Helen Rootham.)

[1] What is my nothingness compared with the stupefaction that awaits you ?

[2] Boole, op. cit., p. 48.

16. Mallarmé and the World of the Sonnets

" Enfin du moi — et du langage mathématique."
(Mallarmé.) [1]

THE world of Mallarmé's poetry offers less difficulty than that of Rimbaud, since the former gives the appearance from the start of being constructed upon the principles of order in the mind. These principles can therefore be used in inquiring into its nature, and this will probably seem a more trustworthy way of going to work than the adoption of the principles of disorder which was necessary in the last two chapters. It must not be supposed from this, however, that Mallarmé's world, the world of the *Sonnets*, is likely to prove any less extraordinary than did that of the *Illuminations*. The world of Logic is quite as queer a place as the world of Nightmare ; its only advantage here is that it has been well mapped.

Since, then, this stage of the inquiry finds itself in the world of Logic, it should be possible to adopt for the moment those normal methods of research which were mentioned in Chapter 11, and begin with analysis and classification of the material in hand. This is a fair sample of the latter :—

" Le noir roc courroucé que la bise le roule
Ne s'arrêtera ni sous de pieuses mains
Tâtant sa ressemblance avec les maux humains
Comme pour en bénir quelque funeste moule." [2]

[1] Quoted by Henri Mondor, *Vie de Mallarmé*, NRF. Gallimard, Paris, 1941, p. 190. (Myself, in short—and mathematical language.)

[2] The black rock angry that the wind rolls it
Will not be stayed even by pious hands
Seeking its likeness to all human ills
As though to bless thereof some tragic mould.
(Translation by Roger Fry.)

It seems at first sight an impossible subject for logical analysis, because, in the words that Mallarmé puts into the mouth of his critics, " la teneur est inintelligible." [1] The fact remains, however, that any Mallarmé sonnet provides all the elements necessary for such an analysis. It is useful to recall Mallarmé's remark to Degas : that poetry is not made with ideas, it is made with words ; and the distinction between the two brings us back to the consideration of language as a double relationship system, sound-look and reference. Mallarmé in that remark throws the emphasis back from the latter to the former, and this is a preliminary indication that the signposts suggested in Chapter 13 for the investigation of Mallarmé's poetry-world may be right. These were the distraction of the mind from reference to sound-look, and the construction from the latter of a relation system, independent of experience, so as to create a world of Nothingness.

Mallarmé himself is, as Rimbaud turned out to be, the best commentator on his methods of procedure. A number of quotations have already been given from his lecture, *La Musique et les Lettres*. The whole of that work is of great importance for this problem, but for the moment it is only the title that matters. Like much else appertaining to Mallarmé, it possesses a certain ambiguity, and it needs to be made plain that the " Lettres " are not intended in the general sense in which, for instance, we use the phrase " men of letters ", or " belles-lettres ". They mean A, B, C, D, the letters of the alphabet, sound-look, in fact. " Un homme peut advenir, en tout oubli — jamais ne sied d'ignorer qu'exprès — de l'encombrement intellectuel chez les contemporains... s'il a, recréé par lui-même, pris soin de conserver de son débarras strictement une piété aux vingt-quatre lettres comme elles se sont, par le miracle de l'infinité, fixées en quelque langue la sienne, puis un sens pour leurs symétries, action, reflet, jusqu'à une transfiguration en le terme surnaturel, qu'est le vers." [2]

[1] From *Divagations*, Le Mystère dans les Lettres. (The purport is unintelligible.)

[2] From *La Musique et les Lettres*. A man may come, in all forgetfulness—it is never fitting to be ignorant save by design—of the intellectual encumbrances of his contemporaries . . . if he has, recreated by himself, taken care to preserve

Valéry speaks of Mallarmé as if the latter in his poetry had been undertaking a piece of research, and says, " The first stage of his research was, of necessity, the defining and production of beauty of the most perfect and exquisite kind. His first task is to determine and separate the elements." [1] The elements, for Mallarmé as well as for us, are groups of sound-look in language which by the hazards of linguistic development have become words, i.e. have become groups fixed by virtue of a constant but arbitrary connection with a particular reference.

Here is chance making an appearance again. There is no need to repeat what has already been said about the mutual exclusion of hazard and poetry in the last chapter. It applies as much to Mallarmé as it did to Rimbaud, but Mallarmé's task of turning the chances of sound-look into necessity is no easier than Rimbaud's. The agencies that in a particular tongue crystallize a certain group of letters round a certain reference and hold it there, thus fixing the primary groupings of sound-look into words, that have produced " cygne " in the French and " swan " in the English, for example, are beyond any poet's control. The phrase " word-music " is sometimes met with in literary criticism, as if it were possible to construct poetry from the sounds alone, conveniently dropping reference by the way. Something of this sort can be written, and an example of it follows, from Mr. De la Mare's *Marching Song* from *The Three Royal Monkeys* :—

" Talaheeti sul magloon
Olgar, ulgar, Manga-noon ;
Ah-mi, Sulâni !
Tishnar sootli maltmahee,
Ganganareez soongalee,
Manni Mulgar sang suwhee,
Sulâni, ghar magleer."

On our definition, however, and Mallarmé's also, this is not poetry, if poetry is words. If a group of sound-look is

from his riddance strictly a piety towards the twenty-four letters as they have, by the miracle of infinity, fixed themselves in some language, his own, then a sense for their symmetries, action, reflection, up to a transfiguration into the supernatural term which is the line of poetry.

[1] *Variété II*, p. 186.

to be a word, the reference must be there also, and attempts at making word-music cannot solve this difficulty, nor is this, as Thibaudet says,[1] what Mallarmé was trying to do.

The answer to the problem is once again contained in Valéry's words quoted in the last chapter, that chance can only be overcome by chance itself, " par l'arbitraire organisé et décrété." The sound-look groupings of words are chance. Could it be possible so to organize these groupings that they would make a system of relations on their own, independent of any reference to experience, a pure web of thought with the words used merely as the " points de rencontre " ? If the product is to be poetry the words will have to be kept unaltered, " les mots — qui déjà sont assez eux pour ne plus recevoir d'impression du dehors." [2] This will mean that each word will bring with it its own reference, but the reference will be for the time being an irrelevance, the interest centring on the construction of a sound-look system of self-sufficient perfection.

Can such a system be found in the Sonnets of Mallarmé ? Three typical examples have been chosen and commentaries upon the results of the analysis follow in each case. (Translations appear in the Appendix.)

FIGURE 5

1 Le silence déjà funèbre d'une moire

2 Dispose plus qu'un pli seul sur le mobilier

3 Que doit un tassement du principal pilier

4 Précipiter avec le manque de mémoire.

[1] Op. cit., Ch. XII, p. 115, " Il est faux. . . que Mallarmé ait conçu la poésie comme une musique."

[2] Mallarmé, *Propos sur la Poésie*, Letter to François Coppée, 5/12/1866, p. 75 (words which already have enough personality to shut out any further impression from outside).

5 Notre si vieil ébat triomphal du grimoire,

6 Hiéroglyphes dont s'exalte le millier

7 À propager de l'aile un frisson familier !

8 Enfouissez-le moi plutôt dans une armoire.

9 Du souriant fracas originel haï

10 Entre elles de clartés maîtresses a jailli

11 Jusques vers un parvis né pour leur simulacre,

12 Trompettes tout haut d'or pâmé sur les vélins,

13 Le dieu Richard Wagner irradiant un sacre

14 Mal tu par l'encre même en sanglots sibyllins.

FIGURE 5

The principal pattern here is the repetition of consonants or vowels at short intervals, indicated by $\overline{3\ \ 3}$ or $\underline{3\ \ 3}$. The vowel a$_2$ provides a double series of internal rhymes, the first on the 6th syllable of lines 1, 5, and 9, the word being a dissyllable in each case, the second in a$_2$l in line 3 at the end, line 5 more in the middle and line 14 at the very beginning. There are also assonance connections with a$_2$ in the middle of lines 10, 11, and 13. In lines 7, 9, and 13 the a$_2$ serves as a counter for the first pattern mentioned, that of repetition. So does the sound e$_1$n, introduced by "sile$_1$nce" in line 1; it continues throughout the sonnet, is twice set in position at the head of the line, and eventually is given a triple repetition, in accordance with the first pattern, in the last line. Two other minor points are worth mentioning: the frequent occurrence of doubled letters, of which there are ten instances here as against an average of 7.4 in eight other sonnets of Mallarmé's examined; and the symmetry of the circumflex accents in lines 8, 10, 12, and 14, indicated by ^{4}

FIG. 6

1 Le vierge, le vivace et le bel aujourd'hui
1 2 3 1 2 1 3 2

2 Va-t-il nous déchirer avec un coup d'aile ivre
1 2 3 2 2 1

3 Ce lac dur oublié que hante sous le givre
2 4 3 2 1

4 Le transparent glacier des vols qui n'ont pas fui!
4 4 5 2 1 2 2

5 Un cygne d'autrefois se souvient que c'est lui
2 6 7 1 2 2

6 Magnifique mais qui sans espoir se délivre
6 2 2 2 4 7 2 1

7 Pour n'avoir pas chanté la région où vivre
1 7 3 4 3 2 1 2 1

8 Quand du stérile hiver a resplendi l'ennui.
4 2 2 1 4 2 4 2

9 Tout son col secouera cette blanche agonie
4 3 5 2

10 Par l'espace infligée à l'oiseau qui le nie,
2 3 7 2 2

11 Mais non l'horreur du sol où le plumage est pris.
3 2

12 Fantôme qu'à ce lieu son pur éclat assigne,
4 2 2 6

13 Il s'immobilise au songe froid de mépris
2 2 2 2 3 7 2

14 Que vêt parmi l'exil inutile le Cygne.
1 2 2 2 2 2 6

FIGURE 6

The essential of this poem is the i_2 pattern. The rhymes make this clear at once, the octet rhyming on ui_2 and i_2vre, the sestet on i_2e and i_2gne. No line is without its i_2 sound. The octet maintains an average of three to a line. In the first line of the sestet it is allowed almost to die out, but is revived by the insistent repetition at the end of line 10, continues (subdued, as other patterns come in here), and finally pegs the pattern home with no less than five repetitions in each of the last two lines.

Added to it is the v_1 pattern. This starts by being intimately associated with the i_2. Of the thirteen occurrences of v_1 in the octet, four are set on both sides of an i_2, in lines 1 and 7. In only three instances is a v_1 separated from an adjacent i_2, and of these, v_1a in line 2 is separated by only two letters from i_2l, v_1ols in line 4 is followed at once by qui_2 while $n'av_1oir$ forms a group with diphthong i_2, for the eye if not the ear, and in any case these last two examples are both drawn into other patterns. The v_1 vanishes in the first five lines of the sestet, to make a solitary reappearance, as a pivot between the five i$_2$ sounds of line 13 and the five of line 14.

The gs make a triple pattern, also linked with the i$_2$ one, hard g$_5$s, of which there are two, in lines 4 and 9 respectively, each time in words of importance and emphasis, with i$_2$ sounds in them ; and soft g$_3$s, to which may be added the ch$_3$s and the one j$_3$. These start in close union with the i$_2$ pattern in four out of their five appearances in the octet. The exception, ch$_3$anté in line 7, begins the variation of the pattern in the sestet, where g$_3$ and ch$_3$ are joined with other vowels, blanch$_3$e, plumag$_3$e, song$_3$e, with Line 10 giving the final dying of the i$_2$g$_3$ connection. Last comes the pattern of the unsounded g$_6$s. Two occur early, in the cy$_2$gn$_6$e and magn$_6$i$_2$fi$_2$que of lines 5 and 6; then they drop out, and are only revived in lines 12 and 14, but here they have the importance of being in the rhyme ending, though unsounded—so the i$_2$ and g$_6$ patterns rejoin at the end, but as it were in silence.

The en$_4$ or an$_4$ sound pattern is particularly noticeable in the octet. In stanza 1 it occurs in the third line, five syllables from the end, followed by repetition in the second and fourth places in line 4. In stanza 2 it occurs in the second line, then in the third line five places from the beginning, then comes its emphasis in the first place of line 8, and then in this same line it reappears in the second and fourth places from the end. In the sestet it occurs twice, in lines 9 and 12 respectively.

A pattern that does not appear till the second stanza is that of oi as a terminating sound. It occurs first as ois in line 5, then changes to oir in line 6, which is repeated in line 7, and then we expect and get a final repetition of oi in the froid of line 13, with a little echo, though not as an ending to a word, in the oiseau of line 10.

Finally there is an echo pattern, the faint echo of ce lac dur in the pur éclat of lines 3 and 12, and the much more solid one of vols, col, sol, in lines 4, 9, and 11, and a half-line internal rhyme in é in lines 2, 3, 4, 7, and 10.

FIGURE 7

1 Ses purs ongles très haut dédiant leur onyx,
1 2 1 3 4 6 6 4 1

2 L'Angoisse, ce minuit, soutient, lampadophore,
1 1 4 1 3 4 2 6 2

3 Maint rêve vespéral brûlé par le Phénix
4 1 2 5 2 1

4 Que ne recueille pas de cinéraire amphore
2 6 1 2

5 Sur les crédences, au salon vide: nul ptyx,
1 6 1 1 1 6 2 3 1

6 Aboli bibelot d'inanité sonore
5 5 5 4 6 3 1

7 (Car le Maître est allé puiser des pleurs au Styx
3 3 2 1 6 2 1 1 3 1

8 Avec ce seul objet dont le Néant s'honore.)
1 1 25 4 6 4 4 1

9 Mais proche la croisée au nord vacante, un or
2 1 7 3

10 Agonise selon peut-être le décor
1 1 2 3 3 6

11 Des licornes ruant du feu contre une nixe,
6 4 6 8 3 1

12 Elle, défunte nue en le miroir, encor
6 8 3

13 Que, dans l'oubli fermé par le cadre, se fixe
6 5 8 6 1 8 1

14 De scintillations sitôt le septuor.
6 1 3 1 1 3 4 1 2 3

FIGURE 7

Here the pattern begins with sibilants. The first two stanzas are introduced by a capital S_1. The rhyme scheme entails an x_1 which brings a sibilant with it, and the or rhyme in lines 6 and 8 adds an s_1 to itself, becoming $s_1$onore and s_1'honore. The average is two sibilants to a line. The exception is line 12, where there is a sudden lapse in the sibilant pattern, giving place to another, and then it is picked up again, so that the last seven words of the poem produce no less than six sibilants.

To counteract what might have been an unduly hissing effect, the poem is very rich in other consonant patterns, all of them being of the kind that catch the eye, p_2 with a shadow pattern of b_5 behind it, t_{34} with a shadow pattern of d_6 behind it, and a sudden burst of f_8 s towards the end. The p_2 pattern is a balance between p_2 s alone, of which the model is set in the opening, S_1es $p_2$urs_1 ongles, and of p_2 s in conjunction with other consonants, of which the pattern is finally brought home in the s_1e$p_2$$t_3$uor of the last line. In the first four lines there are five plain p_2 s to three p_2h groups, but in lines 5–8 and in the sestet the proportion becomes two mixed p_2 s (and mixed with other consonants now, ts and rs and ls) to one plain p_2. This is balanced by a shadow pattern of b_5 s, where the mixed b_5 s of $b_5$rûlé, o$b_5$jet, and ou$b_5$li balance the three plain b_5 s of a$b_5$oli b_5i$b_5$elot.

The t pattern begins inside the important run of the first line, S_1es $p_2$urs_1 ongles $t_3$rès haut_4, and ends inside the similar run in the last line, s_1it_3ôt_4 le s_1e$p_2$$t_3$uor. The sounded t_3 s and unsounded t_4 s are roughly balanced throughout the poem, though the succession of silent t_4 s in line 8 is worth noticing. After $d_6$éfunt_3e in line 12, the t pattern drops out entirely, like the sibilant one, only to be reaffirmed in the last line. There is a shadow pattern of d_6 s behind this, used to close the consonant run of the first line (which has already been mentioned), with its double appearance in d_6é$d_6$iant_4, and to introduce the similar run in the last line, D_6e $s_1$cin$t_3$illations_1. . . . There is one silent d_7, in line 9.

As an echo to the p_2 h sounds of lines 2, 3, and 4 comes the sudden appearance of the f_8 s in lines 11, 12, and 13, serving to frame and emphasize the different nature of these lines, hooking up with the sibilants at each end but continuing through this passage where the sibilants and the t_{34} pattern have both vanished.

Three other details might be mentioned. First, there is the impression that the last phrase, sitôt le septuor, is an echo of the opening one, Ses purs ongles très haut, but more tightly packed, as if a force of physical compression had been exerted on the words in the course of the poem ; secondly, there is the almost anagram-like effect of the two phrases, L'Angoisse ce minuit, and Agonise selon, in lines 2 and 10, even the capital A being preserved, with an attenuated echo in line 8, Avec ce seul, with the capital A again and the repeated sibilant ; thirdly, there is the semi-palindrome effect of the two phrases constructed with the shadow-pattern consonants b_5 and d_6, aboli bibelot and le décor Des licor. . . . Lines 6 and 10–11.

So much for the detailed analysis of the poems. I have by no means exhausted the possibilities of each, but presumably it may be taken that this intricacy of pattern cannot be the product of chance. The very fact that the poems respond so well to this type of investigation is significant, for what has been built up on a logical system can be logically examined. Mallarmé's own words about it become understandable now, and show that he knew exactly what he was doing. Speaking of syntax and its use, he says, " Les abrupts, hauts jeux d'aile, se mireront aussi : qui les mène, perçoit une extraordinaire appropriation de la structure, limpide, aux primitives foudres de la logique." [1] This, with another remark, " Cette visée, je la dis Transposition — Structure, une autre," [2] (this aim I term Transposition—Structure is another), will illustrate the consciousness of the constructive process ; but the nature of the structure comes out clearly, too, in such words as these, " Semblable occupation suffit, comparer les aspects et leur nombre tel qu'il frôle notre négligence : y éveillant, pour décor, l'ambiguïté de quelques figures belles, aux intersections... Chiffration mélodique tue, de ces motifs qui composent une logique, avec nos fibres." [3] Here we have Number and Logic, explicitly. The whole of *La Musique et les Lettres*, indeed, the whole of Mallarmé's prose writings begin to appear no longer obscure but exceedingly illuminating. So, too, does Valéry's comment on Mallarmé, " In this—and I told him so one day—he approached the attitude of men who in algebra have examined the science of forms and the symbolical part of the art of mathematics. This type of attention makes the structure of expressions more felt and more interesting than their significance or value. Properties of transformations are worthier the mind's

[1] From *Divagations*, Le Mystère dans les Lettres. (Sudden and lofty wing-strokes will be mirrored there also : whoever practises them, perceives an extraordinary appropriation of the structure, limpid, to the elemental lightning-shafts of logic.)

[2] Ibid., Crise de Vers.

[3] *La Musique et les Lettres.* Such an occupation suffices, to compare appearances and their number as it may brush across our negligence: awakening there, for decor, the ambiguity of some beautiful figures, at the intersections. . . . Melodic ciphering in silence, of those motifs which make up a logic, with our fibres.

attention than what they transform ; and I sometimes wonder if a more general notion can exist than the notion of a ' proposition ' or the consciousness of thinking no matter what."[1] This is another way of saying what has already become apparent from the analysis of the poems : that the principle of construction of this poetry is to use the elements not for any intrinsic meaning but to mark positions in a relation system. This was so with Rimbaud also ; but in Mallarmé's poetry the system consists of sound-look, and is organized upon the principles of similarity and succession as they appear in Number and Logic.

It is not difficult to see how this works out in the case of Number. Nothing could be much more numerical than the sonnet form which Mallarmé uses, the fourteen lines split into eight and six, with two rhymes repeating at regular intervals in the octet and usually three in the sestet, and the twelve syllables of the alexandrine dividing into smaller numbers according to their own rules. There is a rigid framework of Number, and this is no accident. Mallarmé himself speaks of " l'antique vers, auquel je garde un culte "[2] (the traditional verse-line, for which I cherish a cult). The strict maintenance of a one-by-one, a numerical succession, marked by similarities of sounds at numerically regular intervals—this seems normal enough, and so it is. We are used to Number in poetry, but not to Logic, and this needs to be examined further.

" The *premises* of any logical argument express *given* relations among certain elements . . . the *conclusion* must express an *implied* relation among those elements or among a part of them, i.e. a relation implied by or inferentially involved in the premises."[3] Words are the premises here, this being poetry, with the given relations of sound-look resulting from their fixity in regard to reference. A collection of words may be haphazard, but if they give rise to the notion of some principle of order in the mind, they may be logically examined. Wittgenstein says " Logical research means the investigation of *all regularity* ".[4] Valéry, too, has something to say about this, " combinations displaying

[1] *Variété III*, p. 28.
[2] Preface to *Un Coup de Dés*.
[3] Boole, op. cit., p. 8.
[4] Op. cit., p. 173, 6.3.

regularity, be they in time or space, are irregularly distributed over the field of our investigation. In the mind, they appear to be in opposition to a quantity of formless things." [1] Now, Figures 5–7 produce evidence of ordered and regular combinations of elements, and of these, Valéry goes on to say: "They represent *continuity*. This word is not used here in the mathematical sense. . . . I am concerned only with naive intuition, with objects that remind one of laws—laws that are apparent to the eye. The existence or the possibility of similar things is the first *fact*, and not the least astonishing, of this order." [2] Here, in fact, are succession and similarity again. They are the implied relation [3] among the given elements, as witness Figures 5–7, where the whole analysis turns on the establishment of them. This, then, is the nature of Mallarmé's poems, and it explains their apparent incomprehensibility. "The obscurity found in his work is the result of some kind of rigour which he maintains in all its strictness, rather in the same way as it may happen in science that logic, analogy, and the pursuit of coherence lead to things being presented wholly differently from the ordinary way which has become familiar to us by immediate observation, even to the point of producing *expressions* which deliberately outstrip our powers of imagining." [4] The relations pursued have nothing to do with the reference side of language, as is only right and proper in a system of logic. Mallarmé says the same thing: "Tout écrit, extérieurement à son trésor, doit, par égard envers ceux dont il emprunte après tout, pour un objet autre, le langage, présenter, avec les mots, un sens même indifférent : on gagne de détourner l'oisif, charmé que rien ne l'y concerne, à première vue." [5] "J'extrais ce

[1] *Variété*, p. 237.

[2] Ibid., p. 238 and footnote.

[3] The fact that the relations aimed at are implicit and not explicit may account for the fact, noted by Scherer, that Mallarmé's poetry shows a very great preponderance of nouns over verbs, the latter's usual function being that of *stating* relations.

[4] Valéry, *Variété II*, pp. 216–7.

[5] *Divagations*, Le Mystère dans les Lettres. Everything written, apart from its treasure, must, out of consideration for those from whom it borrows, after all, for a different purpose, the language, present, with the words, some sense even if indifferent : one gains by deflecting the casual reader, charmed that nothing concerns him, at a first glance.

sonnet, auquel j'avais une fois songé cet été, d'une étude projetée sur la *Parole* : il est inverse, je veux dire que le sens, s'il en a un (mais je me consolerais du contraire grâce à la dose de poésie qu'il renferma, ce me semble), est évoqué par un mirage interne des mots mêmes." [1] It now remains to be seen what effect this has on the reader's mind.

The normal function of language is, as we have seen, to provide units for the mind to think with, units to which have been attached particular units of experience in the mind, and from which can be constructed a world that corresponds exactly with the world of experience. Rimbaud and Mallarmé, as all users of language must, preserve the connection between sound-look and reference. Rimbaud used normal words and normal syntax to construct a world that did not conform to the mind's usual organization of experience. Mallarmé works a little differently. His words, like those of Rimbaud, are on the whole ordinary ones, but the syntax is not ordinary. The order of the words, considered as bearers of reference, is most baffling. The mind understands the references individually in such lines as :—

> " Quelle soie aux baumes de temps "...

> " Qui criait monotonement
> Sans que la barre ne varie
> Un inutile gisement
> Nuit, désespoir et pierrerie "...

> " Nubiles plis l'astre mûri des lendemains "...[2]

[1] *Propos sur la Poésie*, Letter to Henri Cazalis, 18/7/1868, p. 83. (The sonnet referred to is that analysed in Fig. 7.) I have taken this sonnet, about which I was thinking this summer, from a projected work on the *Word* : it is inverse, I mean that the sense (if it has one, but I should console myself with the contrary thought thanks to the quantity of poetry which it contains, it seems to me) is evoked by an internal mirage of the words themselves.

[2] " What silk with the balms of time. . . ."

" Which cried monotonous
Though the helm veered not
A useless vein-lode
Night, despair, adamant. . . ."
(Roger Fry's translation.)

" Nubile folds of the future's ripened star."
(Roger Fry's translation.)

but the familiar succession of the words is dislocated, and the mind cannot organize the individual references into a larger group. It is left with a world which has fallen apart into a collection of individual references between which no connecting principles of similarity and succession can be established, and such a world means nothing. But since this is poetry, and therefore a world of words, this is another way of saying that the words as here assembled mean nothing. Rimbaud worked his purpose by using language to make the mind lose its sense of separateness and run everything into one, a total unification. Here, the opposite happens. A tightly organized relation system in the sound-look results in the total disorganization of the reference, and Nothing holds together—quite literally. It would not work if the sound-look groups used were just gibberish ; the process depends for the creation of Nothingness upon there having been something there originally, which seems to vanish, a positive Nothingness, not a negative one.

Now we know how a universe of Nothingness can be constructed from language, and with this knowledge comes the realization of what precise and helpful comments Mallarmé's own words are in this matter. " Signe ! au gouffre central d'une spirituelle impossibilité que rien soit exclusivement à tout, le numérateur divin de notre apothéose, quelque suprême moule qui n'ayant pas lieu en tant que d'aucun objet qui existe : mais il emprunte, pour y aviver un sceau tous gisements épars, ignorés et flottants selon quelque richesse, et les forger." [1] " Appuyer, selon la page, au blanc, qui l'inaugure son ingenuité, à soi, oublieuse même du titre qui parlerait tout haut : et, quand s'aligna, dans une brisure, la moindre, disseminée, le hasard vaincu mot par mot, indéfectiblement le blanc revient, tout à l'heure gratuit, certain maintenant, pour conclure que rien au delà et authentiquer le silence." [2] " Le silence

[1] *Divagations*, Crayonné au Théâtre, Solennité. Sign ! at the central gulf of a spiritual impossibility that nothing should exist exclusively to everything, the divine numberer of our apotheosis, some supreme mould which does not exist in so far as any object exists : but he borrows, in order to burnish a seal there all scattered veins of ore, unknown and floating according to some treasure, and to forge them.

[2] Ibid., Le Mystère dans les Lettres. To insist, according to the page, on

y demeure, précieux, et des signes évocatoires succèdent, pour l'esprit, à tout littérairement aboli." [1]

The world of experience is abolished, and by that destruction the mind is left free to construct its own universe of perfect abstraction. But this, like any other universe, is in the mind, as Mallarmé knew to his cost. " I admit, moreover, but to yourself alone, that the humiliation of my triumph has been so great that I still find it necessary to look at myself in this mirror if I am to be able to think, and that if it were not there in front of the table where I am writing this letter to you, I should revert to Nothingness. This is to let you know that I am impersonal now, no longer the Stéphane Mallarmé you knew—but an aptitude which the Universe of the Spirit possesses for seeing and developing itself, through that which was once myself." [2] If the universe is in the mind and is a universe of Nothingness, the mind cannot retain its own sense of somethingness, of being somebody. Just as in Rimbaud's universe the mind lost its sense of separateness and became everything, so here the mind by its consciousness of separateness, of nothing holding together, must identify itself with Nothingness. The passage from *La Musique et les Lettres*, quoted as an apparent paradox in Chapter 5, ceases to be one now : " d'après quelque état intérieur et que l'on veuille à son gré étendre, simplifier le monde." It has, indeed, become infinitely and terrifyingly simple. Logic is one of the ways to infinity, as Nightmare was.[3] Mallarmé speaks of it plainly : " But mercifully, I am wholly dead, and the least impure region in which my spirit can venture is Eternity—my spirit, that anchorite haunting its own purity, now no longer obscured by the least glance of Time." [4] Rimbaud confronted us with a

the white space, which inaugurates a simplicity, on its own, forgetful even of the title which would speak too loud : and when there aligned itself, in a breach, the least, disseminated, chance conquered word by word, infallibly the whiteness returns, gratuitous earlier, now certain, to conclude nothingness beyond and authenticate silence.

[1] Ibid., Quant au Livre. Silence remains there, precious, and evocative signs succeed, for the spirit, to everything literarily abolished.

[2] *Propos sur la Poésie*, Letter to Henri Cazalis, 14/5/1867, p. 78.

[3] Cf. Havelock Ellis, op. cit., ch. x, p. 278, " Dreaming is thus one of our roads into the infinite. And it is interesting to observe how we attain it—by limitation."

[4] *Propos sur la Poésie*, p. 78.

universe of total everythingness and simultaneity. Mallarmé confronts us with a universe of total nothingness and eternity, and this, too, as we saw in Part I, is no less a vanishing point for the mind than total disorder.

If this is reality and simplicity, it will be a relief to leave it, be it in the form of Everythingness or Nothingness, and come to the change of partners, the movement towards the centre and away from these two extremes, which is represented by two other works of Rimbaud and Mallarmé, *Bateau Ivre* and *Un Coup de Dés*.

17. Bateau Ivre and Un Coup de Dés

" The naked hulk alongside came,
And the twain were casting dice."

(*The Ancient Mariner.*)

IT may at first sight seem strange to set these two poems side by side for the purpose of a sustained comparison. Rimbaud's *Bateau Ivre,* written in 1871, precedes the *Illuminations,* while *Un Coup de Dés Jamais N'Abolira le Hasard* (A Throw of the Dice will never do away with Chance), to give it its full title, was Mallarmé's last work ; it was written in 1897 and the poet died in 1898. Separated by twenty-six years, the first a long poem of twenty-five quatrains of regular form, written by a sixteen-year-old, the second a protracted experiment, twenty-one pages long, in typography and prose poetry, the enigmatic conclusion to the work of a poet of fifty-five, these poems seem to possess little or nothing in common. As has already been seen, however, extremes may bear resemblances the one to the other, and so it is here.

There are certain external points of likeness which can be noticed and then put on one side. First, both poems are considerably longer than the individual *Illuminations* and *Sonnets* ; secondly, each is acknowledged to be highly original ; thirdly, each has been regarded as the peak of its author's achievement.[1] With this it might be supposed that resemblances, superficial or otherwise, come to an end ; on the contrary, they are only just beginning.

The two poems were originally chosen as a good finishing point for this study because they seemed to offer a way back from the extreme horizons of the *Illuminations* and the

[1] Cf. Valéry, *Variété II,* Chapter on *Un Coup de Dés,* q.v. pp. 193–202. Also Dr. Starkie, op. cit., Chapter on *Bateau Ivre*, pp. 138–147.

Sonnets to something nearer the centre of the mind and of language and experience. The preliminary evidence lies in the fact that in these works the two poets seem, so to speak, to change partners, and the Rimbaud who wrote the prose *Illuminations* produces the regular rhymed quatrains, while the Mallarmé who wrote the *Sonnets* produces an experiment in free verse or prose poetry.[1] Rimbaud wrote other poems in regular verse, and Mallarmé, too, has a number of prose poems to his credit, so *Bateau Ivre* and *Un Coup de Dés* are not total exceptions, and are perhaps all the more valuable as evidence for that reason ; but they offer a more balanced and less extreme standpoint from which to survey the respective universes of the poetry of Rimbaud and Mallarmé, because here for the first time we shall be concerned with both form and content, i.e. with sound-look and reference, equally and simultaneously. In fact, what these poems say promises to be interesting. This brings its own difficulty with it, because the question immediately follows : What do they say? They both have a reputation for obscurity, *Un Coup de Dés* very understandably so. The best plan will be to attempt no premature or protracted interpretation of either poem, but to deal with the bits that fit in as we go along, and leave the rest to fall into place in time.

The principal link between these two poems is the figure of the ship which appears in each. In *Bateau Ivre* this is apparent from the title, but in *Un Coup de Dés*, too, the second page gives us the phrase, " Du fond d'un naufrage " (from the bottom of a shipwreck), and the ship makes its appearance in the next two pages ; Mallarmé says of the poem, " Le vaisseau y donne de la bande, du haut d'une page au bas de l'autre." [2]

The result of this is a further bond between the poems, for a fair amount of the vocabulary coincides, brought in by the figure of the ship at sea. A number of examples

[1] Mallarmé, Preface to *Un Coup de Dés*, " reconnaissons aisément que la tentative participe, avec imprévu, de poursuites particulières et chères à notre temps, le vers libre et le poème en prose." (Let us admit frankly that the experiment is akin, unexpectedly, to pursuits peculiar and dear to our age, the free verse-form and the prose poem.)

[2] Letter to André Gide, quoted by Valéry, *Variété II*, p. 200. (The ship is tacking, from the top of one page to the bottom of the other.)

follow, the first in each pair being from *Bateau Ivre*, the second from *Un Coup de Dés* ; the italics are mine.

" L'eau verte pénétra ma *coque* de sapin "
" ...la *coque*
d'un bâtiment
penché de l'un ou l'autre bord "

" Des *écumes* de fleurs ont béni mes dérades "
" ...s'ensevelir
aux *écumes* originelles."

" Libre, fumant, monté de *brumes* violettes "
" faux manoir
tout de suite
évaporé en *brumes* "
" De *la mer* infusé d'astres et lactescent "
" *la mer* par l'aïeul tentant ou l'aïeul contre la mer "

" Plus léger qu'un bouchon j'ai dansé sur les *flots* "
" en maniaque chenu
la partie
au nom des *flots* "
" Et d'ineffables *vents* m'ont ailé par instants "
" comme on menace un destin et les *vents* "

" Sous *l'horizon* des mers..."
" de *l'horizon* unanime."

So a common thread runs through both poems, but the interest lies not in the words but in the metaphor itself, the figure of the ship at sea, isolated in the midst of a vast universe. The sense of isolation is plain in each of these poems, embodied in the " plume solitaire éperdue " of *Un Coup de Dés* which apart from the one word " sauf " has a whole page to itself, and in *Bateau Ivre*, where the loneliness comes out in the first two verses :—

" Comme je descendais des Fleuves impassibles,
Je ne me sentis plus guidé par les haleurs :
Des Peaux-Rouges criards les avaient pris pour cibles,
Les ayant cloués nus aux poteaux de couleurs.

> J'étais insoucieux de tous les équipages,
> Porteur de blés flamands ou de cotons anglais.
> Quand avec mes haleurs ont fini ces tapages,
> Les Fleuves m'ont laissé descendre où je voulais." [1]

One may tentatively make the identification here of ship and soul—a normal figure in poetry—and the result promises to be interesting. We have already been admitted by certain other poems of Mallarmé and Rimbaud to their universes, but it looks as if these two longer poems will give us not only admission to the universe in question, but the spectacle of the poet himself in each case inside his own universe, the mind brooding on its own creation, moving upon the face of the waters. The two things to be investigated next are how far these two poem-universes conform to the patterns we have already traced, and what difference it makes to have the poet there as well, explicitly inside—and at the mercy of—the universe of his own making.

Taking *Bateau Ivre* first, we begin to see very soon that here, as in the *Illuminations*, we have to deal with a universe of everythingness. Rickword says of it, " This poem strained to the uttermost to create out of books of adventure, science, travel, newspapers, and his own sensuous perceptions, a phantasmagoric universe," [2] while Dr. Starkie comments, " He was a *voyant* and he would sail immediately in his mad boat—for it was his right—into the very kingdom of the future. It was here and now he would scale the heights of Heaven and plumb the depths of Hell ; here and now, in this life, he would see everything, hear everything, experience everything." [3] This is familiar ground by now, a universe of everythingness. The interesting thing about this poem, however, is that an inventory of this everythingness, so to

[1] As I came down from the impassive Rivers
I felt myself no longer guided by the men on the ropes :
The noisy Red-Skins had taken them as targets,
Having nailed them naked to the colour-masts.

I was heedless of all the crews,
Carrying Flemish grains or English cottons.
When the hurly burly ended with the sailors,
The Rivers let me descend where I wished.

[2] Op. cit., ch. xii, p. 130.

[3] Op. cit., ch. xii, p. 142.

speak, can be drawn up after a study of the poem. One starts by noticing smaller things, such as the profusion of colours scattered through the poem :—

"J'ai rêvé la nuit verte aux neiges éblouies"...

"Et l'éveil jaune et bleu des phosphores chanteurs."

"Planche folle, escorté des hippocampes noirs,
Quand les Juillets faisaient crouler à coups de triques
Les cieux ultramarns aux ardents entonnoirs."

"Libre, fumant, monté de brumes violettes,
Moi qui trouais le ciel rougeoyant comme un mur."

"Glaciers, soleils d'argent, flots nacreux, cieux de braises,
Échouages hideux au fond des golfes bruns."

"J'aurais voulu montrer aux enfants ces dorades
Du flot bleu, ces poissons d'or"...[1]

Once one begins to look into it, one is astonished at the contents of this universe. There are men, women, and children :—

"Des Peaux-rouges criards"...
"Et je restais ainsi qu'une femme à genoux"
"Moi, l'autre hiver, plus sourd que les cerveaux d'enfants."[2]

[1] I have dreamed the green night with the dazzled snows

And the yellow and blue awakening of the singing phosphorescence.

Mad plank, escorted by black seahorses,
When the Julys brought down by cudgel-strokes
The ultramarine skies with the glowing funnels.

Free, smoking, lifted by violet mists,
I who riddled the sky reddening like a wall

Glaciers, silver suns, pearly waves, skies of embers,
Hideous runnings aground down brown gulfs

I would have wished to show to children these dolphins
Of the blue water, these fishes of gold

[2] Noisy Red-skins
And I remained so, like a woman on her knees
I, the other winter, deafer than the brains of children

All the five senses are here, sight, hearing, touch, taste (both food and drink), smell :—

> " J'ai vu fermenter les marais, énormes nasses "
>
> " Je courus ! et les Péninsules démarrées
> N'ont pas subi tohu-bohus plus triomphants."
>
> " Baisers montant aux yeux des mers avec lenteur "
>
> " ...confiture exquise aux bons poètes "
> " Plus fortes que l'alcool..."
> " Choient des arbres tordus avec de noirs parfums." [1]

Here are beasts,

> " Mêlant aux fleurs des yeux de panthères." [2]

reptiles and insects,

> " ...les serpents géants dévorés des punaises." [3]

birds,

> " L'aube exaltée ainsi qu'un peuple de colombes " [4]

sea-creatures,

> " Où pourrit dans les joncs tout un Léviathan "
> " ...ces poissons chantants " [5]

flowers, trees, and other growing things, " ses fleurs d'ombre," " des arbres tordus," " Des lichens de soleil " (its flowers of shadow ; twisted trees ; lichens of the sun).

[1] I have seen the marshes fermenting, enormous lobster-pots

I ran ! and the unanchored peninsulas
have not undergone a more triumphant hurly-burly.

Kisses mounting to the eyes of the seas slowly

. . . exquisite jam for good poets
Stronger than alcohol...
Fall from twisted trees with black perfumes.

[2] Mingling with flowers the eyes of panthers

[3] Giant serpents devoured by bugs.

[4] Dawn exalted like a race of doves

[5] Where in the reeds a whole Leviathan rots
These singing fish.

The background of nature is here in every possible manifestation, lightning, tempest, whirlwind, electricity, phosphorescence, waterspouts, whirlpools, glaciers, snow, rivers, waterfalls, the Poles and the Tropics. Lastly, there is a colossal geography, so to speak, starting with details, " Péninsules," " récifs," " golfes," but ending with great masses, "J'ai heurté, savez-vous ? d'incroyables Florides " (I have, do you know ? run against unbelievable Floridas), and "Je regrette l'Europe aux anciens parapets " (I regret Europe of the ancient parapets). But this is not all, for the geography extends into the sky, as did the voyage of the *bateau ivre*, as if sun and stars were but more distant Americas waiting to be explored,

> " J'ai vu des archipels sidéraux, et des îles
> Dont les cieux délirants sont ouverts au vogueur : "

This last point is perhaps the most important of all, for it gives us a clue to the relation between the ship and the sky it sails under, or sails by, or sails in, and this may be a clue to Rimbaud's relationship to his own universe. There will be more to say about this in a moment, when we have considered the universe of the Mallarmé poem.

In *Un Coup de Dés* we should expect to find emptiness if the universe of this poem is to conform to the universe already discovered in the *Sonnets*. Certain preliminary indications point that way. Mallarmé says, in his Preface to the poem, " Les ' blancs ' en effet, assument l'importance, frappent d'abord " (indeed, the white spaces take the initiative and make the first impression) ; while Valéry says of it, " My vision came to grips with silences that had, as it were, become incarnate." [1] The poem itself bears this out. The figures used in it, the dice, the sea, the ship, the individual, the ambiguous " plume " (pen or feather), the stars, are all as much attenuated as possible. As the Preface says, " Tout se passe, par raccourci, en hypothèse ; on évite le récit " (Everything takes place, by foreshortening, in hypothesis ; the direct account is avoided). The dice appear only as a *throw* of the dice, " QUAND BIEN MÊME LANCÉ DANS DES CIRCONSTANCES

[1] *Variété II*, p. 194.

ÉTERNELLES " (even if thrown in eternal circumstances). The figure of the ship comes in first as " DU FOND D'UN NAUFRAGE ", the ship lost, in fact. The sea makes its appearance like this :—

" SOIT
que
l'Abîme
blanchi
étale
furieux
sous une inclinaison..." [1]

and sea and ship combine into a shadowy vision of something suspended precariously between upper and nether abysses :—

"l'ombre enfouie dans la profondeur par cette voile alternative
jusqu'adapter
à l'envergure
sa béante profondeur en tant que la coque
d'un bâtiment
penché de l'un ou l'autre bord..." [2]

The individual enters as " LE MAÎTRE ", followed closely by the words " Esprit " (spirit)—where the body has gone, " cadavre " (corpse) where life has gone, " maniaque "—where reason has gone. On the last page come the stars, but they come in as " UNE CONSTELLATION ", the emphasis being on their arrangement rather than on themselves, and even this becomes at once the abstract oı " un compte total en formation " (a sum total in formation), just as the dice of the beginning re-enter in abstract form in the last line, " Toute Pensée émet un Coup de Dés," the movement of the dice becoming a movement of thought.

The use of abstract phrases, of what Valéry calls " an abstract noun, invariably empty " (*Variété*, p. 266), is most

[1] Be it that the Abyss, whitened, displays, furious, beneath an inclination...

[2] shadow buried in the depths by this alternative sail
to the point of adapting
to the fullspread of sail
its gaping depth in proportion to the hull
of a ship
listing to one side or the other

noticeable throughout, " DES CIRCONSTANCES ÉTERNELLES," for instance, or " *Une insinuation simple au silence enroulée avec ironie* ", " *une borne à l'infini* ".[1] So also are the recurring notions of Number, Chance, and Probability, " L'unique Nombre qui ne peut pas être un autre " (the unique Number which can be no other), " LE HASARD," " cette conjonction suprême avec la probabilité " (this supreme conjunction with probability). Another feature is the use of words explicitly or implicitly negative or empty, ranging from small phrases like " *la neutralité identique du gouffre* " (the identical neutrality of the gulf), " *au front invisible* " (with the invisible forehead), " l'inutile tête " (the useless head), " de contrées nulles " (regions of nullity), to bigger groups such as :—

" le voile d'illusion rejailli leur hantise
ainsi que le fantôme d'un geste
chancellera
s'affalera
folie N'ABOLIRA..." [2]

or this :—

" naufrage cela sans nef
n'importe
où vaine " [3]

and eventually to something as sustained as this, which makes up a complete double-page unit :—

" RIEN
de la mémorable crise
ou se fût
l'événement accompli en vue de tout résultat nul
humain

[1] A simple insinuation to silence, rolled up with irony. A boundary to infinity.

[2] the sail of illusion spurted out, their haunting
like the phantom of a gesture
will totter
will draw too near the shore
madness
will not abolish

[3] shipwreck that
without a vessel
no matter
where useless

N'AURA EU LIEU
une élévation ordinaire verse l'absence
QUE LE LIEU
inférieur clapotis quelconque comme pour disperser l'acte vide
abruptement qui sinon
par son mensonge
eût fondé
la perdition
dans ces parages
du vague
en quoi toute réalité se dissout." [1]

This is unquestionably the same Mallarmean universe of emptiness and absence that we have met before, and like *Bateau Ivre*, this poem resolves itself in the end into the problem of the relation between the poet and his universe.

Both these universes are familiar ; but there are two new elements in them as presented in these poems. The first is the presence of the poet himself. The second is the curious and interesting fact, very noticeable in the reading of these poems, that Rimbaud's universe in *Bateau Ivre* is a sunlit one, while Mallarmé's in *Un Coup de Dés* lies under the night sky and the stars. This may seem trivial ; but it is not, because to our relation to the sky, sunlit or starlit, we owe our knowledge of our relations of time and space. Perhaps something may come of examining further the position of each poet in his universe, that position to be logged by the relation between the poet and the heavens above him. In the first case, there is Rimbaud in a universe of everythingness with the sun for landmark, in the second, Mallarmé in a universe of nothingness seeking " the star to

[1] Nothing
of the memorable crisis
or was
the event accomplished in view of every null human result
will take place
an ordinary elevation pours out absence
but the place
inferior rippling of some sort as if to disperse the empty act
abruptly which if not
by its lie
would have founded
perdition
in these coastal waters
of the void
in which all reality dissolves.

every wandering bark ". But in each case the universe is a poem-universe, so the relations will be inside the poem ; we are not concerned directly with the philosophy of either poet, merely with an organization of words in a couple of poems.

In studying the *Illuminations* we saw how the words were organized so as to make the mind forget the limitations of sound-look—hence also the limitations of normal experience, including space-time relations—and lose itself in the simultaneous everythingness of Nightmare. In *Bateau Ivre* things work differently. The organization of the words, as sound-look, is different, and this is going to affect the relations of the universe constructed—for here Rimbaud has not abandoned Number. Number is kept, in the regular twelve-syllable quatrains, rhyming two and two, and with this goes the sense of Number in the poem ; of Number in time, periods split up and organized on a numerical basis, " dix nuits " (ten nights), " des mois " (months), " les Juillets " (the Julys) ; of Number applied to Space, " sentant geindre à cinquante lieues " (hearing groaning fifty leagues away) ; of Number ruling a universe of separate things making a total but capable of enumeration, so that, as we have seen, the contents of this universe of everythingness can be catalogued one by one. This is a universe which the mind still holds in control by the principles of Number, and this prevents the final simplification, the identification of the mind with its own universe, which happens in *Les Illuminations*.

The mind is still separate from its time-keeper and landmark in this universe, the sun, and so is still able to measure time and space by it. This holds good for the first seventeen verses of *Bateau Ivre*, which consist of the description of the progress of the ship through its own universe ; but with the last eight verses something happens, described in verses 18–21 which form a group unseparated by full-stops at the end of the verses. The three most important are given below :—

> " Or moi, bateau perdu sous les cheveux des anses,
> Jeté par l'ouragan dans l'éther sans oiseau,
> Moi dont les Monitors et les voiliers des Hanses
> N'auraient pas repêché la carcasse ivre d'eau,

Libre, fumant, monté de brumes violettes,
Moi qui trouait le ciel rougeoyant comme un mur
Qui porte, confiture exquise aux bons poètes,
Des lichens de soleil et les morves d'azur,

* * *

Moi qui tremblais, sentant geindre à cinquante lieues
Le rut des Béhémots et des Maelstroms épais,
Fileur éternel des immobilités bleues,
Je regrette l'Europe aux anciens parapets." [1]

At this point in the poem the *bateau ivre* becomes air-borne, and, so it seems to me, starts heading straight for identification with the sun, but taking its sea with it, into one final union of mind and universe. One might suppose that this is the same process as that which holds good in the *Illuminations* ; but it is not, because this universe differs by having the mind of the poet, here the ship, in it. It is the mind of the poet which is sucked up into the sun, not that of the reader. The subject of the experiment is the poet. The reader, because this universe is still presented to him in a form organized and kept separate by Number, can preserve his own detachment, whatever happens to the poet. But for this very reason it now becomes possible to see more clearly what happens to the poet on whom this extraordinary experiment is carried out. The last three verses of *Bateau Ivre* suggest that it was a failure, with the dejection of :—

[1] Now I, a ship lost beneath the tresses of the bays,
Thrown by the hurricane into the birdless air,
I whom the Monitors and the sailing-ships of the Hansa
Would not have dredged up again, a carcase drunk with water,

Free, steaming, borne by violet mists,
I who riddled the sky reddening like a wall
That bears, exquisite jam for good poets,
Lichens of the sun and the snot of the blue sky,

I who trembled, feeling the groaning fifty leagues away
Of the rutting of the Behemoths and the thick Maelstroms,
Threading my way eternally through the immobilities of the blue,
I regret Europe of the ancient parapets.

> " Mais vrai, j'ai trop pleuré. Les aubes sont navrantes,
> Toute lune est atroce et tout soleil amer.
> L'âcre amour m'a gonflé de torpeurs enivrantes.
> Oh, que ma quille éclate ! Oh que j'aille à la mer ! " [1]

But the last line here suggests that the desire for identification was still there, though expressed in a different way, and the final verse expresses the poet's sense of inability to return to normal ways and normal shipping-lanes again :—

> " Je ne puis plus, baigné de vos langueurs, ô lames,
> Enlever leur sillage aux porteurs de cotons,
> Ni traverser l'orgueil des drapeaux et des flammes,
> Ni nager sous les yeux horribles des pontons ! " [2]

This conclusion suggests not that Rimbaud " knew now his wild journey was over and he must content himself with everyday reality ", as Dr. Starkie says (ch. xii, p. 145), but the exact contrary, the intention to try again ; and if so, *Bateau Ivre* is a remarkable indication and interpretation of what was to come. Chance phrases that Rimbaud wrote later on spring to one's mind and begin to acquire a new significance.

" J'avais, en effet, en toute sincérité d'esprit, pris l'engagement de le rendre à son état primitif de fils du Soleil."

(*Illuminations*, Vagabonds.)

" J'aimai le désert, les vergers brûlés, les boutiques fanées, les boissons tiédies. Je me traînais dans les ruelles puantes et, les yeux fermés, je m'offrais au soleil, dieu de feu."

(*Une Saison en Enfer*, Alchimie du Verbe.)

" Enfin, ô bonheur, ô raison, j'écartai du ciel l'azur, qui est du noir, et je vécus, étincelle d'or de la lumière *nature*."

(Ibid.) [3]

[1] But, truly, I have cried too much. The dawns are harrowing,
Every moon is hateful and every sun bitter.
Acrid love has swollen me with intoxicating torpors.
O that my keel might burst ! O that I might go back to the sea !

[2] I can no longer, bathed with your langours, o waves,
Cut off their wash from the freighters of cotton,
Nor traverse the arrogance of the flags and flames,
Nor swim beneath the horrible eyes of the pontoons !

[3] " In all sincerity I had promised to restore him to his primitive state of ' Child of the Sun '."

(Translation by Helen Rootham.)

I loved the desert, burned up orchards, faded shop-awnings, drinks grown

But the most surprising thing of all is the poem which immediately follows this last passage in *Une Saison en Enfer*, also included as one of the verse poems in the *Illuminations*, for it looks as if once again Rimbaud is to be taken literally at his word, and the poem begins to make sense. I give the variant which Rimbaud gives in *Une Saison en Enfer*, because it makes the point better :—

> " Elle est retrouvée !
> Quoi ? l'Éternité.
> C'est la mer mêlée
> Au soleil.
>
> Mon âme éternelle,
> Observe ton voeu
> Malgré la nuit seule
> Et le jour en feu
>
> Donc tu te dégages
> Des humains suffrages,
> Des communs élans !
> Tu voles selon...
>
> Jamais l'espérance,
> Pas d'*orietur*.
> Science et patience,
> Le supplice est sûr.
>
> Plus de lendemain,
> Braises de satin,
> Votre ardeur
> Est le devoir.
>
> Elle est retrouvée !
> — Quoi ? — l'Eternité.
> C'est la mer mêlée
> Au soleil." [1]

tepid. I dragged myself through the stinking alleys and, eyes closed, offered myself to the sun, the god of fire.

At length, o joy, o reason, I pushed back from the sky its blueness, which is darkness, and I lived, a spark of gold of the light, *Nature*.

[1] It is found again !
What ? Eternity.
It is the sea mingled
With the sun.

The poem speaks for itself in the clearest possible manner. The union of the ship, which is Rimbaud, and the sun and the sea is finally dissolved in the later section of *Une Saison en Enfer*, Adieu.

" L'automne déjà ! — Mais pourquoi regretter un éternel soleil, si nous sommes engagés à la découverte de la clarté divine, — loin des gens qui meurent sur les saisons.

L'automne. Notre barque élevée dans les brumes immobiles tourne vers le port de la misère, le cité énorme au ciel taché de feu et de boue.

* * *

— Quelquefois je vois au ciel des plages sans fin couvertes de blanches nations en joie. Un grand vaisseau d'or, au-dessus de moi, agite ses pavillons multicolores sous les brises du matin... Eh bien ! je dois enterrer mon imagination et mes souvenirs !

...je suis rendu au sol, avec un devoir à chercher, et la réalité rugueuse à étreindre ! " [1]

My eternal soul,
Observe thy vow
Despite the lonely night
And the day on fire

Therefore thou detachest thyself
From human suffrages,
From common aims !
Thou fliest accordingly. . . .

Never any hope,
No *orietur*.
Wisdom and patience,
Torture is certain.

No more to-morrow,
Fire-glow of satin,
Your ardour
Is duty

It is found again !
What ? Eternity.
It is the sea mingled
With the sun.

[1] Autumn already ! But why regret an eternal sun, if we are engaged upon the discovery of the divine light,—far removed from the people who die upon the seasons.

Autumn. Our barque uplifted in the motionless mists turns towards the harbour of misery, the enormous city with the sky stained with fire and mud.

—Sometimes I see in the sky endless beaches covered with white nations rejoicing. A great vessel of gold, above me, flutters its many-coloured pennons in the breezes of morning. . . . Oh well, I have got to bury my imagination and my memories.

. . . I am let down to earth, with a duty to look for, and rugged reality to be embraced !

But in *Bateau Ivre* the final apotheosis and downfall are still in the future. Sun, ship, sea, and poet are still separate, and by the use of the principle that Mallarmé employs to construct *his* universe, Number (hence the remarks made earlier about the change of partners), everythingness is organized and made visible in time, while the necessary detachment of the reader from the universe he is surveying is left intact. We are visitors in a vision, not, as in the case of the *Illuminations*, prisoners in a nightmare. This world does no violence to the mind. What is to come casts its shadow before, for we see that the *bateau ivre* cannot prolong indefinitely its nicely balanced voyage of poetry between sea and sky, earth and infinity, time and eternity ; but for a space we are content to say with the poet, " I have seen all the works that are done under the sun," and to forget that the sentence ends, " and behold, all is vanity and vexation of spirit."

It is time now to turn to the other ship, in its own setting of sea and sky—Mallarmé and the stars. The figure of the constellation at the end of *Un Coup de Dés* is the most important piece of evidence here, but not the only one. Valéry's chapter on this poem in *Variété II* connects up with the stars again and again. " There, on the paper itself, there trembled I know not what infinitely pure scintillation of ultimate stars in that same empty space between two consciousnesses where, like some new species of matter, distributed in groups, in trails, in systems, *coexisted* the Word ! " " He has tried, I thought, *to raise at last a page to the power of the star-filled sky* ! " [1] Three other quotations are also relevant, two from Mallarmé himself, the third from Coppée's journal :—

" ...l'incohérent manque hautain de signification qui scintille en l'alphabet de la Nuit." [2]

(*Divagations*, Crayonné au Théâtre, Ballets.)

" Tu remarquas, on n'écrit pas, lumineusement, sur champ

[1] Pp. 195 and 199.
[2] the haughty incoherent lack of significance which scintillates in the alphabet of the Night.

obscur, l'alphabet des astres, seul, ainsi s'indique, ébauché ou interrompu ; l'homme poursuit noir sur blanc." [1]

(Ibid., Quant au Livre.)

" Mallarmé devient plus fou que jamais... La lune le gêne. Il explique le symbolisme des étoiles, dont le désordre dans le firmament lui paraît l'image du hasard." [2]

(Quoted by Mondor, op. cit., p. 328.)

One may deduce that Mallarmé saw an analogy between the way letters are grouped into words and the way stars are grouped into constellations. Both appear to be the result of hazard ; how then can the poet make them into necessary combinations, the intersections of an order of relations in the mind ? The order in the mind which we have explored in the *Sonnets*, and which was built up by Number and Logic, bore no relation to experience. Here something else will be needed if the application of words to constellations, or the alphabet of letters to the alphabet of the Night is to be brought about. So we find that Mallarmé, in his turn, abandons Number, regular verse, and the normal linear one-by-one succession of words, and adopts instead the principle of simultaneity which hitherto we have met with only in Rimbaud's universe, the universe of Dream and Nightmare. Because this is a poem-universe, these new relations of space-time have to be created by the organization of the words, and from this follow the strange typographical effects of *Un Coup de Dés*. Valéry has given an account of the double function of any collection of words, of which the following is an extract : " But beside and apart from reading itself, everything written exists and subsists from the point of view of a whole to be looked at. A page is a picture. It gives a general impression, displays a block or a system of blocks and strata, of blacks and whites, more or less happy in form and intensity. This second *way of looking at things*, no longer successive and

[1] You remarked, one does not write, luminously, on a dark ground, the alphabet of the stars, alone, thus is indicated, outlined or interrupted ; man pursues black on white.

[2] Mallarmé grows madder than ever. . . . The moon bothers him. He explains the symbolism of the stars, whose disorder in the firmament seems to him the image of chance.

linear and progressive as reading is, but immediate and simultaneous, means that typography can be compared with architecture, just as, earlier on, reading might have brought to mind melodic music and all the arts that espouse time." [1] The unusual disposition of the type in *Un Coup de Dés* achieves the dislocation of those space-time relations which, as Valéry points out, belong to normal reading, and by emphasizing " une vision simultanée de la Page ", as Mallarmé says in the Preface to the poem, allows the world of Dream to enter in place of the world of Number, and permits the unification in the imagination of the words scattered about the page with the stars scattered about the night sky. The poem, to run together the sentence in capitals which is separated by interpolations in other forms of type, says " SI C'ÉTAIT LE NOMBRE CE SERAIT LE HASARD " (if it were Number it would be Chance)—but it is not Number any more, and so a new necessity is formed, " un compte total en formation," and with it comes a new significance. It is not, as in the *Sonnets*, that all reference, and hence all experience, is abolished, but that the unification of groups of letters and groups of stars lends to each a new significance. But here again, as with *Bateau Ivre*, the reader can remain detached, and can watch from this detachment the identification of words and stars.

The effect of both *Bateau Ivre* and *Un Coup de Dés* upon a mind that has lost itself in those other universes of the *Illuminations* and the *Sonnets* is extraordinary. They are not merely, as these last-named works are too, exciting and beautiful ; they carry with them also a profound sense of consolation and reassurance which it is difficult to account for unless the mind perceives here some greater balance. Everythingness and nothingness are here, too, but in *Bateau Ivre* Rimbaud's universe of everythingness is made subject to the mind by being dealt with in linear fashion, lengthened out and shown by the principles of Number to consist of a succession of familiar elements drawn from experience, so that in a good sense " there is nothing new under the sun ", while Mallarmé's universe of nothingness is made subject to the mind by the identification of the elements through the

[1] *Pièces sur l'Art*, p. 18.

18. Conclusion

> " I saw three ships come sailing in."

THE last chapter was headed by a couple of lines from the *Ancient Mariner*, which by an interesting chance unite two of the principal figures of the poems that have just been considered, the *bateau ivre*, a " naked hulk " if ever there was one, and the *coup de dés*, the casting of the dice. Now this may be nothing more than a coincidence, but the more one thinks about it, the more does it seem as if this uniting of the two images may be a pointer to other and more far-reaching connections.

Coleridge has already made his appearance in this study. His words on the logic of poetry were quoted in Chapter 14 ; he was familiar with dreams, speaking of " a dream world of phantoms and spectres, the inexplicable swarm and equivocal generation of motions in our brains " (*Biographia Literaria*, vol. i, ch. 8) ; and his theory of the imagination still keeps literary critics busy—or keeps them guessing. So he himself is no stranger. But the sudden irruption of *his* ship into this study, at the very end, when there seemed little more to do than summarize the results, was strange and surprising. For now there are not two ships, Rimbaud's wild boat and Mallarmé's shadowy vessel : there are three. The Ancient Mariner's ship is coming sailing down the long sea-lane between these other two ships that hold their courses on their respective horizons ; and this third ship steers a middle course, for language and poetry, between the other two.

Early in this study it was recognized that Mallarmé and Rimbaud might represent two extremes, attempting the impossible, trying to pull away from the central regions of the mind towards their opposite infinities. It was this that made them easier to study, and the middle regions of the mind have on the whole been avoided, because they would plainly need a study all to themselves which could be undertaken only after the extremes had been mapped. Now, however, with this vision of the three ships, we shall have to look at the middle more carefully. In what is to be the last chapter of this book, I cannot attempt the sounding of this great central tract of sea where the Ancient Mariner sails. All that can be done is to look at the ship, so to speak, and to plot its position not in relation to the spaces in which it moves (which must wait for further study) but in relation to the other two ships with which we are now reasonably familiar, as also with the universes in which they move. For these three may be looked at as three types of poetry, three ways in which the mind may voyage, with a greater or lesser degree of safety, across these uncertain waters.

It is as if the two lines of progress of the two outlying ships could be plotted (we saw in the last chapter that they seemed to constitute a movement back towards the more central space of the mind) ; and at the point of intersection of the two tracks might lie the third ship's position.

The general characteristics of each of the two French poems were, briefly, the dominant figure of the ship, the sense of loneliness and the solitary wrestling with the universe in which the voyage took place. All these may be found in the *Ancient Mariner* :—

> He holds him with his skinny hand,
> " There was a ship," quoth he.
>
> Alone, alone, all, all alone,
> Alone on a wide, wide sea !
>
> But the sky and the sea, and the sea and the sky
> Lay like a load on my weary eye,
> And the dead were at my feet.

The characteristics of the universe in which Rimbaud's ship moved were : the introduction of Number, and of time and space divided numerically, the profusion of colours, of living things of all kinds, of sunlight, of terrestrial and celestial geography of infinite variety and on a huge scale. All these can be found too in the Coleridge poem. This produces Number, pure and applied :—

> Four times fifty living men . . .
> Under the keel nine fathom deep . . .
> Like April hoar-frost spread . . .
> In the leafy month of June. . . .

There are human beings, the crew, the hermit, the pilot, and the pilot's boy,

> Old men and babes and loving friends
> And youths and maidens gay,

animals, birds and reptiles, a horse, a wolf, the albatross, the skylark, the owlet, the water-snakes. There are colours,

> As green as emerald . . .
>
> Through fog-smoke white . . .
>
> The water, like a witch's oils,
> Burnt green, and blue, and white.
>
> Her lips were red, her looks were free,
> Her locks were yellow as gold :
> Her skin was white as leprosy . . .
>
> Blue, glossy green and velvet black . . .
>
> And thy skinny hand so brown.

There is sunlight :—

> The western wave was all a-flame,
> The day was wellnigh done.
>
> Nor dim nor red, like God's own head,
> The glorious Sun uprist :
>
> The Sun came up upon the left,
> Out of the sea came he !

but it is worth noticing, too, that the moon is in this poem also, quite as frequently. There is an enormous geography, embracing Tropics and Poles, and something, too, of that fusion of earth and sky which one met in *Bateau Ivre*,

> The thick black cloud was cleft, and still
> The Moon was at its side ;
> Like waters shot from some high crag,
> The lightning fell with never a jag,
> A river steep and wide.

This was the Rimbaud universe. The Mallarmean one had for its background " A darkness of stars And a foaming of spray ". It was a sum of negatives, of a spirit, a corpse, a maniac. These are all here, too ; the *Ancient Mariner* is full of Spirits ; there are corpses in plenty, and at the end someone " doth crazy go ". It has a crew with " limbs like lifeless tools ", a curiously exact echo of the Mallarmé phrase, " cadavre par le bras " ; it has a " spectre-bark ", and the throw of the dice ; it has starred nights ; there seems even a parallel between the " plume solitaire éperdue " (agitated solitary quill), a feathered thing which has taken more definite shape in the Coleridge poem and appears as an albatross, which at first " voltige autour du gouffre " (flutters around the gulf), or, as Coleridge puts it, " And round and round it flew " and in the end " Choit... aux écumes originelles " (falls into the original foam) :—

> The Albatross fell off, and sank
> Like lead into the sea.

So this third ship holds the balance between the other two, not by detaching itself from them but by embodying in itself the characteristics of each, and making from them what is perhaps a more perfect equilibrium. Once again it is a question of balance, that notion that has kept recurring here. This final balance may be looked at in four ways—and then we have done.

First, there is the balance of the poem itself, the *Ancient Mariner*. This is attained in the way that has been discussed earlier, and put forward as probably the normal organization for language in poetry : the ordering of sound-look according to the principles of Number, and of reference according to the principles of Dream. The ways in which this balance and organization may vary must be countless, but the general pattern should hold good for all poems that do not, as those of Rimbaud and Mallarmé did, attempt to pull out of this field altogether.

Secondly, there is the balance of the Ancient Mariner's ship in its universe. This seems to be achieved by perpetual movement, and this also fits with the suggestion made earlier that equilibrium in this central region of the mind could only be unstable and brief, to be attained " not by fixity but by movement ", as T. S. Eliot says. In this poem everything is constantly moving ; sun, moon, stars, day running headlong into night (" No twilight in the Courts of the Sun ", as Coleridge says himself in one of the marginal notes), the wind blows, the ship flies along ; even the dead men rise and start to move about. There is a horror of fixity here, the terror of being becalmed,

> Day after day, day after day,
> We stuck, nor breath nor motion ;
> As idle as a painted ship
> Upon a painted ocean,

the horror of enforced bodily inaction, the imprisonment in a human frame,

> Seven days, seven nights, I saw that curse,
> And yet I could not die,

the worse horror of the immobile tongue,

> With throats unslaked, with black lips baked,
> We could not laugh nor wail ;
> Through utter drought all dumb we stood !

This leads on to the third point, the maintenance of equilibrium in the mind—for it is done by language. The Ancient Mariner from time to time has to *put his story into words*, to call in language to exorcise the intolerable strain of some overwhelming experience (common, as far as one can judge, to the Rimbaud and the Mallarmé poem as well). Coleridge, however, encases it in further words, supplying a marginal commentary and giving the story a narrator, so that it may seem to the mind no more than " a tale that is told ". It upset the Wedding Guest, since " He went like one that hath been stunned, And is of sense forlorn ", but the reader is insulated one degree more from the dangers of the forces at work here as in all poetry apparently.

Fourthly, there is the equilibrium in the poet's own mind. At the end of these three long poems, the balance should have been achieved in each case. Mallarmé ends, "Toute Pensée émet un Coup de Dés," leaving us with the stars held steady, even if only for a moment, in a mind. Rimbaud ends, "Je ne puis plus..." as if the equilibrium here were the enforced relaxation of exhaustion. Coleridge ends, surprisingly and, to some, shockingly with a moral, so simple, almost banal, with its introduction of prayer and the love of God, that it has been disclaimed as out of place. But it is not. Earlier, two other things besides poetry were suggested as holding the balance in the mind between order and disorder, rejoicing in both. The one was laughter—so that the Jumblies' boat and the ship in *The Hunting of the Snark* will follow a slightly different route, which in time I hope also to follow up. But Coleridge calls in the other, which was religion, leaving us centred there, as the poem ends its progress down the middle line of language and experience where poetry has its fair and proper place.

APPENDIX

The three following translations are by Helen Rootham :

FIG. 2.

CHILDHOOD—III

In the wood there is a bird ; his song checks you and makes you blush.

There is a clock which does not strike the hour.

There is a bog in which is a nest of white beasts.

There is a cathedral which comes down, and a lake which goes up.

There is a little carriage standing forsaken in the underwood ; or it comes down the path at a run, decked with ribbons.

There is a troupe of little actors in costume ; one just sees them on the road which skirts the wood.

And last of all, if you are hungry or thirsty, there is someone who chases you.

FIG. 3.

FLOWERS

Seated on a golden stair—amongst silken cords, grey gauzes, green velvets, and crystal disks which blacken in the sun like bronze—I watch the foxglove open on a ground of filagree-work of silver, eyes and hair.

Pieces of yellow gold lie scattered upon the agate, mahogany pillars support a dome of emeralds, white satin bouquets and slender twigs of rubies encircle the water-lily.

Like a blue-eyed god sculptured in snow, the sea and the sky draw to the marble terraces the crowd of strong young roses.

FIG. 4.

AFTER THE FLOOD

As soon as the idea of the Flood had abated

A hare paused in the clover and shaking bell-flowers, and prayed to the rainbow through the spider's web.

What jewels gleamed in hiding—what flowers gazed about them.

In the dirty high-street sprang up the stalls, and boats were dragged towards the sea, staged above it as in old prints.

Blood washed the walls of Bluebeard's house, flowed in the slaughter-houses and in the circuses, where the windows grew livid beneath the seal of God. Blood and milk flowed.

Beavers built up their houses. Glasses of black coffee steamed in the little wine-shops.

In the great house of glass still streaming with water, children dressed in mourning looked at the marvellous pictures.

A door banged ; and in the village market-place the child waved his arms to answer the vanes and the weathercocks on all sides, under the glittering spatter.

Madame X set up a flat in the Alps. Masses and first Communions were celebrated at the hundred thousand altars of the cathedral.

Caravans set off. And the Hotel-Splendide was built in the chaos and night at the Pole.

Since then the moon has listened to the jackals whining in thyme-scented deserts—and eclogues in sabots grunting in the orchards. Then in the violet forest all a-burgeon, Eucharis called me, saying " It is spring ".

Brim over, o pool ; foam, roll over the bridge, and cover the forests ; sable cloths and organs, lightnings and thunder, rise up and roll ; waters and sorrows, rise and lift up the floods again.

Because since the floods fell, precious stones have so buried themselves, and flowers so opened in profusion, that it has become an untellable boredom ! And the Queen, the Sorceress, who kindles her glowing embers in the earthen pot, never will she consent to enlighten our ignorance.

FIG. 5.

The silence already funereal of a moire
Disposes more than one fold alone upon the furniture
That a subsidence of the principal pillar should
Precipitate with the lack of memory.

Our so ancient triumphal amusement of scribbling,
Hieroglyphics by which the thousand exalt themselves
To propagate with the wing a familiar shiver !
Bundle it rather for me into a cupboard.

Of the original smiling fracas hated
Amongst themselves by lordly lucidities has sprung forth
Towards an outer temple born for their simulacrum,

Trumpets out loud of gold fainted upon vellum,
The god Richard Wagner irradiating a consecration
Ill concealed by the ink itself in sibylline sobs.

The following two translations are by Roger Fry :—

FIG. 6.

This virgin, beautiful and lively day
Will it tear with a stroke of its drunken wing
The hard, forgotten lake which haunts beneath the frost
The transparent glacier of flights unflown !

A swan of past days recalls it is he
Magnificent but without hope who is freed
For not having sung the realm where to live
When sterile winter's ennui has shone forth.

All his neck will shake off this white agony
By space inflicted on the bird who denies it,
But not the horror of the soil where his plumage is caught.

Fantom that to this place his brightness assigns him,
He is stilled in the icy dream of contempt
Which clothes in his useless exile the Swan.

FIG. 7.

Her pure nails very high dedicating their onyx,
Anguish, this midnight, upholds, the lampbearer,
Many vesperal dreams by the Phenix burnt
That are not gathered up in the funeral urn

On the credences, in the empty room : no ptyx,
Abolished bibelot of sounding inanity
(For the Master is gone to draw tears from the Styx
With this sole object which Nothingness honours).

But near the window void Northwards, a gold
Dies down composing perhaps a decor
Of unicorns kicking sparks at a nixey,

She, nude and defunct in the mirror, while yet,
In the oblivion closed by the frame there appears
Of scintillations at once the septet.

SELECT BIBLIOGRAPHY

PRINCIPAL WORKS

STÉPHANE MALLARMÉ. *Divagations.*

—— *Œuvres poétiques.*

—— *Œuvres en Prose.*

—— *Propos sur la Poésie, recueillis et présentés par Henri Mondor.* Editions du Rocher. Monaco, 1946.

JEAN-ARTHUR RIMBAUD. *Œuvres Complètes.*

PAUL VALÉRY. *L'Âme et la Danse.* Gallimard, Paris, 1924.

—— *Charmes.* Gallimard, Paris, 1926.

—— *Eupalinos ou l'Architecte.* Gallimard, Paris, 1924.

—— *L'Idée Fixe.* Gallimard, Paris, 1934.

—— *Mélange.* Gallimard, Canada, 1941.

—— *Monsieur Teste.* Gallimard, Paris, 1927. Nouvelle edition augmentée, 1946.

—— *Pièces sur l'Art.* Gallimard, 1934.

—— *Poésie et Pensée Abstraite.* Zaharoff Lecture for 1939. Clarendon Press, Oxford, 1939.

—— *Variété.* Gallimard, Paris, 1924.

—— *Variété II.* Gallimard, Paris, 1930.

—— *Variété III.* Gallimard, Paris, 1936.

—— *Variété IV.* Gallimard, Paris, 1938.

CRITICAL WORKS

BERRICHON, PATERNE. *Jean-Arthur Rimbaud.* Mercure de France, Paris, 1912.

BRUNETIÈRE, FERDINAND. *Essais sur la Littérature Contemporaine.* Calmann Lévy, Paris, 1892.

COULON, MARCEL. *Le Problème de Rimbaud.* Gomès, Nîmes, 1923.

DANIEL-ROPS. *Rimbaud — Le Drame Spirituel.* Plon, Paris, 1936.

FRANCE, ANATOLE. *La Vie Littéraire,* 2e Série. Calmann Lévy, Paris.

GHIL, RENÉ. *En Méthode à l'Œuvre.* Léon Vanier, Paris, 1904.

HACKETT, C. A. *Le Lyrisme de Rimbaud.* Nizet et Bastard, Paris, 1938.

HURET, JULES. *Enquête sur l'Évolution Littéraire.* Charpentier, Paris, 1913.

KAHN, GUSTAVE. *Symbolistes et Décadents.* Vanier, Paris, 1902.

LEMAÎTRE, JULES. *Les Contemporains*, 4e, 5e, 8e Série. Paris, 1889, 1892, 1918.

MENDÈS, CATULLE. *Le Mouvement poétique français de 1867 à 1900.* Fasquelle, Paris, 1903.

MONDOR, HENRI. *Vie de Mallarmé.* Gallimard, Paris, 1941.

RICKWORD, EDGELL. *Rimbaud : The Boy and the Poet.* Heinemann, London, 1924.

RUCHON, FRANÇOIS. *Jean-Arthur Rimbaud.* Champion, Paris, 1929.

SCHERER, JACQUES. *L'Expression littéraire dans l'œuvre de Mallarmé.* Droz, Paris, 1947.

STARKIE, ENID. *Arthur Rimbaud.* Hamish Hamilton, London, New Edit., 1947.

THIBAUDET, ALBERT. *La Poésie de Stéphane Mallarmé.* Gallimard, Paris, 5th Edit.

GENERAL WORKS

BODKIN, MAUD. *Archetypal Patterns in Poetry : Psychological Studies of Imagination.* O.U.P., 1934.

CAUDWELL, CHRISTOPHER. *Illusion and Reality : A Study of the Sources of Poetry.* Lawrence and Wishart, London, New Edit., 1946.

COLERIDGE, SAMUEL TAYLOR. *Biographia Literaria*, vols. i and ii. Edit. by J. Shawcross, Clarendon Press, Oxford, 1907.

DAY LEWIS, C. *The Poetic Image.* Jonathan Cape, London, 1947.

EMPSON, WILLIAM. *Seven Types of Ambiguity.* Chatto and Windus, London, 1930.

RICHARDS, I. A. *The Interactions of Words.* Essay in *The Language of Poetry*, edit. by Allen Tate. Princeton U.P., 1942.

—— *The Philosophy of Rhetoric.* O.U.P., New York and London, 1936.

—— *Practical Criticism : A Study of Literary Judgment.* Kegan Paul, Trench, Trubner, and Co., Ltd., London, 1929.

—— *Principles of Literary Criticism.* Kegan Paul, Trench, Trubner, and Co., Ltd., London, 1925.

—— *Science and Poetry.* Kegan Paul, Trench, Trubner, and Co., Ltd., London, 1926.

SITWELL, EDITH. *Introduction to Prose Poems from " Les Illuminations " translated by Helen Rootham.* Faber, London, 1932.

LANGUAGE

BALLY, CHARLES. *Linguistique générale et linguistique française.* Leroux, Paris, 1932.

BLOOMFIELD, LEONARD. *Language.* George Allen and Unwin, Ltd., London, 1935.

BRUNOT, FERDINAND. *Histoire de la Langue française des origines à 1900.* Colin, Paris, 1905. Vol. i and vol. viii.

—— *La Pensée et la Langue.* Masson et Cie., Paris, 1922.

DAUZAT, ALBERT. *La Philosophie du Langage.* Flammarion, Paris, 1917.

—— *La Vie du Langage.* Colin, Paris, 1910.

—— *Tableau de la Langue française.* Payot, Paris, 1939.

DELACROIX, H. *L'Analyse psychologique de la Fonction linguistique.* Clarendon Press, Oxford, 1926.

JESPERSEN, OTTO. *Mankind, Nation, and Individual.* Aschehoug, Oslo, 1925.

—— *Language : Its Nature, Development, and Origin.* George Allen and Unwin, London, 1922.

—— *The Philosophy of Grammar.* Allen and Unwin, London, 1924.

MAROUZEAU, J. *Traité de Stylistique.* Paris, 1935.

MEILLET, A. *Les Langues dans l'Europe Nouvelle.* Payot, Paris, 1918.

—— *Linguistique historique et linguistique générale.* Champion, Paris, 1926.

—— *La Méthode comparative en linguistique historique.* Aschehoug, Oslo, 1925.

OGDEN AND RICHARDS. *The Meaning of Meaning.* Kegan Paul, London, 1927.

SCHLAUCH, MARGARET. *The Gift of Tongues.* Allen and Unwin, London, 1943.

VENDRYES, J. *Le Langage,* La Renaissance du Livre, Paris, 1921.

LOGIC AND MATHEMATICS IN GENERAL

AYER, ALFRED JULES. *Language, Truth, and Logic.* Gollancz, London, Second Edit., 1947.

BLACK, MAX. *The Nature of Mathematics.* Kegan Paul, London, 1933.

BOOLE, GEORGE. *An Investigation of the Laws of Thought.* Wilton and Maberly, London, 1854.

CARNAP, RUDOLF. *The Logical Syntax of Language.* Kegan Paul, Trench, Trubner, and Co., Ltd., London, 1937.

—— *La Science et la Métaphysique devant l'Analyse Logique du Langage.* Series : Actualités Scientifiques et Industrielles, No. 172. Hermann et Cie, Paris, 1934.

FREGE, G. *Grundgesetze der Arithmetik.* Pohle, Jena, 1893.

NICOD, JEAN. *Foundations of Geometry and Induction.* Kegan Paul, Trench, Trubner, and Co., Ltd., London, 1930.

POINCARÉ, HENRI. *La Science et l'Hypothèse.* Flammarion, Paris, undated.

—— *Science et Méthode.* Flammarion, Paris, undated.

—— *La Valeur de la Science.* Flammarion, Paris, undated.

RUSSELL, BERTRAND. *Introduction to Mathematical Philosophy.* Allen and Unwin, London, 1919.

—— *The Principles of Mathematics.* C.U.P., 1903.

WEYL, HERMANN. *Philosophie der Mathematik und Naturwissenschaft.* Oldenbourg, Munich, and Berlin, 1927.

WHITEHEAD, ALFRED NORTH. *Modes of Thought.* C.U.P., 1938.

WHITEHEAD AND RUSSELL. *Principia Mathematica.* C.U.P., 1910.

WITTGENSTEIN, LUDWIG. *Tractatus Logico-Philosophicus.* Kegan Paul, London, 1922.

PHYSICS

BRIDGMAN, P. W. *The Nature of Physical Theory.* Princeton U.P., 1936.

CARR, H. WILDON. *The General Principle of Relativity.* Macmillan, London, 1920.

DUNNE, J. W. *The Serial Universe.* Faber and Faber, Ltd., London, 1934.

EDDINGTON, SIR ARTHUR. *New Pathways in Science.* C.U.P., 1935.

—— *The Philosophy of Physical Science.* C.U.P., 1939.

EINSTEIN, ALBERT. *The Meaning of Relativity.* Princeton U.P., 1945.

—— *Relativity : The Special and the General Theory.* Methuen, London, 1920.

HERTZ, HEINRICH. *The Principles of Mechanics.* Macmillan, London, 1899.

JEANS, SIR JAMES. *Physics and Philosophy.* C.U.P., 1942.

JOAD, C. E. M. *Philosophical Aspects of Modern Science.* Allen and Unwin, London, 1932.

MACH, ERNST. *The Science of Mechanics.* Open Court Publishing Co., Chicago, 1893.

PLANCK, MAX. *General Mechanics.* Macmillan, London, 1933.
—— *Wege zur physikalischen Erkenntnis.* Hirzel, Leipzig, 1933.
—— *Where is Science Going?* Allen and Unwin, London, 1933.
RUSSELL, BERTRAND. *Physics and Experience.* Henry Sidgwick Lecture for 1945, C.U.P., 1946.
WATSON, W. H. *On Understanding Physics.* C.U.P., 1938.
WHITEHEAD, ALFRED NORTH. *Science and the Modern World.* C.U.P., 1927.

NUMBER

CANTOR, GEORG. *Contributions to the Founding of the Theory of Transfinite Numbers.* Chicago, 1915.
DANTZIG, TOBIAS. *Number: The Language of Science.* Allen and Unwin, London, 1930.
DEDEKIND, RICHARD. *Essays on the Theory of Numbers.* Open Court Publishing Co., Chicago, 1909.
HARDY AND WRIGHT. *An Introduction to the Theory of Numbers.* O.U.P., 1938.
WEYL, HERMANN. *Das Kontinuum.* Veit, Leipzig, 1918.

DREAM

BERGSON, HENRI. *Dreams.* Fisher Unwin, London, 1914.
BINZ, C. *Ueber den Traum.* Marcus, Bonn, 1878.
DUNNE, J. W. *An Experiment with Time.* A. and C. Black, Ltd., London, 1927.
FREUD, SIGMUND. *On Dreams.* Heinemann, London.
—— *The Interpretation of Dreams.* Allen and Unwin, London, 1913.
—— *Wit and Its Relation to the Unconscious.* Trans. by A. A. Brill. Kegan Paul, Trench, Trubner, and Co., Ltd., London.
GREENWOOD, F. *Imagination in Dreams and their Study.* John Lane, London, 1894.
HAVELOCK ELLIS. *The World of Dreams.* Constable, London, 1911.
HUTCHINSON, H. G. *Dreams and their Meanings.* Longmans Green, London, 1901.
JUNG, C. G. *Psychology of the Unconscious.* Kegan Paul, London, 1921.
SULLY, JAMES. *Illusions.* Kegan Paul, London, 1882.

INDEX

INDEX